AF470609

THE CHAMPIONS

THE CHAMPIONS

Great Racehorses and Show Jumpers of our Time

Judith Campbell

Arthur Barker Limited
London

CONTENTS

ILLUSTRATIONS

Acknowledgements

The author and publishers would like to thank the following for permission to reproduce the photographs: W. W. Rouch & Co. for the jacket photograph of Brigadier Gerard and those of Arkle, Nijinsky and Mill Reef; Syndication International for those of Mill House and Doublet; Central Press Photos for those of Mandarin and Foxhunter; Sport and General Press for those of Aureole, Freebooter and Psalm; Major Allhusen and Sport and General Press for that of Lochinvar; Associated Press for that of Golden Miller; Wilson and Horton Ltd for that of Phar Lap; Photonews and Cecil Covey for that of Indian Magic; Monty for that of Lucky Strike; Alex Gill and Albert Deptford for that of Pretty Polly and Stanley Dancer for that of Albatross.

FOREWORD

A champion is one who excels in his own particular field. A champion horse is the one that, either in the opinion of experts or through its prowess in jumping or racing, hits the top – and each year produces its own crop.

To choose twenty champions, alive or dead, from all the hundreds that can so justly lay claim to the title was no easy task and many will question the absence or inclusion of some 'obvious' animal. Everyone to his own choice; this choice is my own. I have tried to cover as many aspects as possible of all appertaining to the horse, and then to select those animals whose personality makes them, to my mind, stand out from the rest.

Judith Campbell

I
ARKLE

The dictionary defines a freak as a caprice, an eccentric person, a monstrosity even, but when you mention the name Arkle to an Irish stable-lad and he comments, his eyes dreamy, the brogue mellifluous, 'Oh, th'harse was a freak, y'know!', his meaning is a very different one. What he is telling you is that, just as history confirms how at intervals the centuries produce a man larger than life and made for the fame he creates, so the years occasionally engender a horse of comparative stature. Lottery, winner of the 1839 Grand National, was such a one, Arkle was another.

Arkle was out of Bright Cherry, a good but not outstanding 'chasing mare, and by Archive, a horse of Nearco blood that by breeding could have won the Derby but whose racing performance is best forgotten. In Pharos, Arkle shared a common ancestor with his rival, the great horse Mill House, whose story is entwined with his.

He was bred in Ireland, by Mrs. Baker who farms near Greenogue, and was born on 19 April 1957. Her daughter, a famous horsewoman, reared him and broke him, and sold him as a three-year-old at the Ballsbridge Sales in Dublin for 1,150 guineas to the Irish-born Anne, Duchess of Westminster. The Duchess sent her new purchase to Eaton Lodge, her home in Cheshire, and christened it Arkle after the Scottish mountain. When the gelding was four and a half,

Tom Dreaper, the Irish Trainer, came over to choose between him and the much better looking Brae Flame, a horse of the same age. Intuition may have had something to do with the trainer's decision to pick Arkle, but chiefly it was a sentimental allegiance to Bright Cherry, that he had trained, with many of her family, and all the more admirable since the mare's distance was two miles on good going – a very unlikely dam of a three-mile 'chaser that liked the mud. There was no great flurry of excitement over the arrival of the newcomer at the Dreaper stables at Kilsallaghan.

The horse looked big and gaunt; to the Head Lad he appeared the worst of all the four-year-olds; to his future jockey, Pat Taaffe, a youngster that neither looked like a good horse nor moved like one. Arkle was consigned to the new stable lad, a sixteen-year-old called John Lumley who never learned to ride that horse or any other, but was to have the pride and pleasure in the seasons to come of turning out a champion 'looking like a picture'.

Arkle quickly settled to the routine of a stables where care is taken to see the horses do not suffer from boredom. He learned to accept with calm interest the sudden descent of a cloud of racing pigeons, the extensive progeny of a pair that appeared out of the sky one day, and that perch as of right on the blue-blooded heads and valuable backs of young horses soon indifferent to their presence. If there was a sudden thump on his stable door from a football during the lads' lunch-hour, Arkle ignored what quickly became a normal part of the absorbing enjoyment of watching humans at play. Everything was interesting, and everyday episodes of this kind helped to ensure that even the most temperamental young horses were less likely to become upset by untoward incidents. Arkle's daily exercise took in, in turn, all the fields on the Dreapers' farm. He became used to every kind of going, to slopes and turns at walk and trot and canter, with, later, a circuit or two, perhaps twice a week, at a contained gallop, all of which helped to balance him physically and kept him mentally occupied.

From the start he took to the little training fences that he jumped first from the end of a lunge at a slow canter, and later with an experienced lad, but until January 1962 the best that anyone hoped for Arkle was that he might eventually win a steeplechase or two.

His initiation into 'chasing was done in the normal manner of Ireland, starting with two little bumper races on the flat, both in December 1961. He finished third in the first, over two miles on tough going that proved he could stay, and came fourth in the other against better class horses. Hurdling was the next step, and in the following January when he was five, Arkle was entered as a complete outsider in a three-mile novice hurdle at Navan. When, still in comparatively low gear, he cruised past the twenty-seven runners, to win at 20-1, nobody knew quite what had hit them, and even then they had no inkling of what the future was to hold. The horse's next three efforts at hurdling, hard ridden by Pat Taaffe to get another win, to finish unplaced – for the only time in his career – then to achieve only a fourth, were not very illuminating either.

For the Duchess, Arkle was always a pet, loved for himself even more than for his prowess, and in that first summer that he spent in leisure on her Bryanstown farm near Maynooth, when his future was still an unknown quantity, she began to know the horse as a character, apart from his mission in life. Even then he was a study in contradictions, and had a total and engaging trust in humans. He would come home, after months in hard training, still not totally relaxed and 'let down', and if resting when the Duchess visited him in the stable, would lie and 'converse' with her, without even bothering to get up. At Bryanstown, where he was to spend all the summer holidays of his racing career, he was to be found, a relaxed mound of brown-haired horseflesh, stretched flat out at his ease in the gentle sunshine and graciously willing to make the effort to lift his head and nuzzle sugar from her hand. As the racing game became more familiar, the preparations beforehand, little items such as plaiting his mane, were so perfectly understood that Arkle would expend nervous energy as soon as the process began, 'on his toes' a couple of hours before the start. So to fool him they learned to let his mane go free, and so contain the excitement until it was time almost for the 'off'. Even at exercise his competetive spirit would boil up at a moment's notice, and Pat Taaffe will not forget the day with Arkle when he and Flyingbolt, both of them by then immensely valuable 'chasers, cooked up a private race between them over schooling fences, and ensured they would never be risked together like that again. Yet in the stable, with his owner, with his lad, with his work-rider, with children, visitors, fans, his donkey friend, his dog companion, Arkle was kind and quiet, friendly and always a gentleman. There are few horses of his trade and calibre that could be ridden bareback at a garden party. Yet this is what Pat Taaffe did, best suit and all, when Arkle came to greet his guests at a reception given for him by the Duchess in the garden that adjoins his paddock at Bryanstown, after his peak season of 1964.

Arkle always summered well, and after his first holiday came out in October '62 to impress Pat Taaffe, when he rode him to a six-length win at Dundalk. That same month Arkle was seen for the first time in England. In good company, and ridden by the stable work-rider, Paddy Woods, he took the important President's Handicap Hurdle at Gowran Park, and gave the British sports writers food for thought and comment.

The horse tended to jump like a greyhound, hind legs landing outside his forelegs, which gave him speed but he frequently cut himself in the process. That day at Gowran Park the wound inside his hock was a deep one, but was nothing compared with what he might have done to himself soon afterwards, when warming up over hurdles preparatory to a school over fences near Fairyhouse racecourse. As it happened it was Pat Taaffe who bore the brunt that day, with a damaged eye that had to be stitched, but the crashing fall Arkle took through carelessness over the second flight, ending up with forelegs shoved through the bars, is the manner in which many horses have finished their lives with a broken leg. Yet in a way it was a god-send. Arkle was far too intelligent to make the same mistake twice, and though he was to hit plenty of fences and occasionally seemed to be heading for dire trouble, he would always fiddle his way out of it somehow – and he never fell again. He concluded that 1962 season by winning the Honeybourne Chase at Cheltenham by twenty lengths, over big fences and against useful horses. That was when Pat Taaffe finally awoke to just what kind of a horse they were keeping there at the yard at Kilsallaghan. That was the moment when the whispered query 'Gold Cup winner?' was first breathed, the moment when Arkle could be considered as a serious contender for the Mill House crown.

Between February 1963 and the following October, Arkle won all six of his races, two in England, the rest in Ireland with one of them on the flat. In November he was to meet Mill House at Newbury in the Hennessey Gold Cup, for the duel that the racing and non-racing fraternity alike had been waiting for.

This was the first of the rounds between the giants, and the result can be interpreted according to which camp you are in – Mill House adopted for England, Arkle for Ireland. Mill House was leading four fences from last, with Arkle second and closing on him. At the next, the open ditch, something happened – Pat Taaffe said Arkle stood off a long way but cleared the fence all right to slip, forelegs outstretched, on landing; a bystander said the horse's foot went into a hole made by other racing hooves; someone else thought he blundered before landing; but whatever it was he checked, and the race was lost. To those who knew and loved Arkle, it was unbelievable. To the Mill House contingent it was a clear-cut victory, the best horse giving away five pounds in weight to win.

That was December '64. The next round would be the top-liner, the Cheltenham Gold Cup in March. In the meantime Arkle came out at Leopardstown to cut down to size a fancied National runner amongst the field, and win by two lengths. By now he was carrying the big weight of twelve stone, but he took the valuable Thyestes Chase at Gowran Park the next month by eight lengths, and after his nearest challenger fell at Leopardstown a few weeks later, came home to win in a canter.

Mill House had not been wasting his time either, and had two easy wins, one of them the King George VI, to his credit.

At Cheltenham that day in 1964 there were only two others to take on the giant-killers, both good horses, both starting at long odds to dramatise the gulf between 'good' and 'champion'. But the four of them moved down to the start, and the sun came out and chased away the snow flurries, and the crowds, keyed to fever pitch, had eyes only for the two brown horses. 'Himself' as they entitled him in the country he hailed from, and the handsome 'Big Horse', the champion for England, who was in fact, for all his huge dimensions, smaller than his rival.

Mill House, jumping beautifully, took the lead and held it, with

Arkle, pulling hard, six or so lengths behind. That is how it went until they were coming to the second to last when Arkle started to close the gap, and then, with Pas Seul toiling far behind with King's Nephew, both the unwilling chorus to the two principals, he landed, passed Mill House and galloped away. As easy as that.

He won the Irish Grand National the same month, and after that the Irish Stewards changed the handicapping rules to try and encompass this one horse. From then on there was one lot of weights for races that included Arkle, and another lot for occasions when he was absent. It was better than what the Clerk of the Course did to Lottery in 1840. He thought up a Grand Steeplechase, a sweepstake with the enticing prize of 25 sovereigns with 100 added – but ensured his field, that would not have lined up against a 'cert' like Mr Elmore's horse, by making it open to all . . . except Lottery.

When Arkle and Mill House next met – after the summer holiday of 1964 and a victory that October in the Carey's Cottage Handicap Chase – Arkle was carrying what could have been a crippling 12st 7lb. This time, at Newbury, he chose not to leave Mill House out in front – his jockey always maintained that Arkle made most of the decisions himself – and for that Hennessey Gold Cup the tactics were certainly his own. So he made his way alongside the Big Horse, matching each beautiful jump, however big, with one as good or better, until Mill House was stretched to the limit and could do no more. Then Arkle went on alone over the last two fences to win, leaving his great rival to labour in to an unaccustomed and dispiriting fourth place.

To outjump another horse until he broke its heart was the outcome of Arkle's competetive spirit on more than one occasion, and without it diminishing his position as the pride and darling of the public, there was still the occasional headline to suggest that lesser horses were ruined by his invincible superiority.

A week after the Hennessey Gold Cup and carrying yet another 3lb as the penalty of victory, Arkle ran in the Massey-Ferguson, and was just beaten into third place. Even freaks have their limitations, and this one was then given a three month rest.

There was a hard won race at Leopardstown in February 1965 as preparation for Cheltenham. Then a month later it was on to the

Gold Cup again with only Mill House to count – and when the Big Horse twice blundered badly Arkle had only to canter in and collect.

By now 'Himself' was a handsome creature, a proud, courageous horse, with great depth through the heart and powerful sloping shoulders as his most obvious physical qualities. A hidden strength lay with one of the slowest recorded heartbeats. He had won £36,818, and was on his way to a further six wins in a row. They were to include an appalling mistake at the fourth fence in the Whitbread Gold Cup, that never even checked him, another devasting twenty-four-length win over Mill House when conceding 16lbs at Sandown, and the hardest race of his life to beat a little mare at Leopardstown.

Joining the élite, the only other three winners of the Gold Cup ever to start at odds-on – and Arkle was at 10-1 on – he courted disaster at Cheltenham that year by inattention, and took the last fence first time round with his chest. Impossibly, he survived and to discount the concerted conviction that he was going to fall, took his third consecutive Gold Cup in a canter, thirty lengths ahead of a field where one had been killed, and another was too exhausted to be ridden from finishing post to unsaddling enclosure.

After that little effort Arkle was off the course for six months before turning out at Newbury. There the going was heavy, he was carrying two stone more than all five of his opponents bar one, and he was beaten by half a length into second place by Stalbridge Colonist, a doughty son of Sir Winston Churchill's famous Colonist II. A month later, on 14 December 1966, Arkle remedied that omission by winning the SGB Handicap Chase at Ascot by what was almost an insolent fifteen lengths. From his dedicated public he got the kind of ovation that he loved and had come to expect, the acclamation normally reserved for pop stars, and only Pat Taaffe failed fully to appreciate the scene. He knew that horse like he knew himself, and for all the ease of the win he sensed that there was just something amiss with Arkle's action. With any racehorse this is the constant fear, with the Arkles of this world (if such there be), it might seem like tempting providence not to follow up even the haziest of premonitions. But no-one could find anything wrong at all and the horse showed not the suspicion of a limp. So, with ears pricked and eyes bright with the sheer enjoyment of the game, the champion came to line-up for the King George VI Chase at Kempton Park.

Arkle was 9-2 on, and in a field of seven, Woodland Venture at 6-1 seemed the only member of the opposition to have any support at all, but in the event he and the 10-1 Dormant were in the picture up to the last fence. Arkle, game as always, was holding them and clear as he jumped the last. Then Dormant came up to him stride by stride and Arkle failed by a length.

It seemed to many that day that Arkle's jumping lacked his usual brilliance, and when he made a mistake at the open ditch and hit the guard-rail, hard, that was probably the moment when the trouble his jockey had sensed came to a head, and he finished that race, still battling, with a broken bone in his foot. Only a horse of superlative courage would have gone on in the increasing pain.

The X-rays confirmed the fracture in the pedal bone, that lies behind the wall of the hoof and south-east of the navicular bone, a more frequent cause of trouble. Arkle's own vet put the leg in plaster, and his own stable lads took turns to look after him, and he stayed on at Kempton Park for the next six weeks, treated with all the care, and given the prestige of the VIP he was. Special bulletins kept his public informed of progress, each post brought him his own 'mail', and each day he enjoyed a bottle of the stout prescribed by his vet, and sent him by an admirer.

When the plaster was removed Arkle was flown home to Ireland, back to Tom Dreaper's stables, to the good care of his lad Johnny Lumley, and of Paddy Woods who rode him. As far as the foot was concerned it was a question of time.

After nearly two years the foot was as good as new, and the question then was one of policy, of ambition, and, the most important, of affection. The news, and the public were always optimistic. Arkle would make his come-back. First, he would have his re-introduction in February 1968 at Leopardstown, in the Restoration Stakes, on the flat over two miles. Then there was firm public belief that he would come to England in 1969 to make a bid for his fourth Cheltenham Gold Cup. In fact Arkle never raced again. He had been off the racecourse for two years and it's no easy matter to make a come-back after that length of time, even for a young horse. He was still fresh and saucy and at exercise Paddy Woods had a job to restrain him, but Arkle was ten, eleven, and his owner loved him. Perhaps there was a great temptation to prove this champion of all champions could still do it, but the Duchess said he should leave while still at the peak, and there was never a better decision.

But before he came home to her at Bryanstown, to grow plump and shining on the good grass and spend his last days in contentment, Arkle did come to England. With the Duchess and Tom Dreaper, with Paddy Woods to attend him and Pat Taaffe to jump back in the saddle, he was flown in to appear at the Horse of the Year Show when it celebrated its twenty-first birthday in October 1969. And as the focal point of each evening Arkle, the star – head up, eyes shining, reacting to the thunderous applause with the same old pride and delight – was ridden by his jockey, Pat Taaffe, in the Duchess of Westminster's famous colours, to steal the limelight from all the others in the Personality Parade of the show that year.

For Arkle the band played 'There'll never be another you'. He won £75,207 in prize money, and he took 'chasing's most coveted prize, the Cheltenham Gold Cup, back to Ireland three years running. Because of that broken bone he never had the chance to improve on Golden Miller's five successive victories, but it is Pat Taaffe's conviction that, barring his accident, Arkle would have won the next three Cups with ease. The Duchess would not risk her horse in the National, so again the Miller remains one up – and again Arkle's jockey contends that the horse had such brilliance, that he was so clever a jumper and possessed of such speed and stamina, that, given the necessary luck, the Grand National would have been no problem.

That is surmise and we shall never know. Arkle is dead. He spent his days happily until the moment it was realised his foot was giving pain, then there was a swift decision to save him more, and he was put down.

But the Age of Arkle was the Golden Age of Steeplechasing, and his courage and character, linked to his racing brilliance, reached out through television to capture a huge following in both Ireland and England. Perhaps his like will never be seen again. Maybe a 'freak', in the Arkle sense, will turn up in years to come, but it will take a long, long time to produce another horse like that.

2
MILL HOUSE

In the end, if only for a little while, Mill House returned to hunting. Then the back that could be painful one time and not the next, and the unsound legs – those physical disabilities that had dogged the big horse through the latter part of his racing career – made him a not too safe conveyance in the hunting field. So although the old gentleman remains, as he will to the end of his days, loved and cosseted amongst the comforts and beautiful setting of Peter Walwyn's training stables, his exercise is now taken in the form of gentle hacking.

Hunting, in the capable hands of Pat Taaffe, with the Kildare, or the South County or Naas Harriers, was part of Mill House's early training. It was galloping across country with hounds, when gates and ditches and walls all came alike to him, that he first showed that soaring brilliance of jumping that was to capture and hold his racing public, and make his rider describe him as 'something to fill the mind of a man'. And in some respects, with his huge frame and broad back, Mill House looked more like a hunter than anything else. As a young, green horse turned out in a field, it was only when he moved that you saw the 'chaser in him and realised hunting was not his proper *métier*.

As with most young 'chasers in Ireland, and particularly if trained by someone like Tom Taaffe, Pat's father, hunting was a normal part of the programme, because it teaches a horse to be keen and clever. Before that phase Mill House had already done a little preliminary schooling over hurdles and small fences with Pat, who always rode him at work. After the hunting they moved on quickly to more serious matters, and the memory of those days with hounds, combined with the ease and speed with which the big horse came to hand, convinced his rider that this was one that could be the horse of the century; a feeling sustained by the manner of Mill House's running when they won together, first time out.

And for all the blunder that ended his next race at the fourth flight, in an important champion novice's hurdle, there were others who shared Pat's view, and Mill House's performance was considered sufficiently impressive to bring the Epsom trainer, Syd Dale, hot-foot to Ireland with Mr Gollings, a prospective buyer, in tow.

So Mill House came to England, and until retirement his life was encompassed by the routine of a trainer's yard. After little more than a year he had exchanged Syd Dale's yard for that of Fulke Walwyn, but although the methods of different trainers may vary a little, the basics that fill a 'chaser's day remain the same. If Mill House was one of the horses on first exercise, then it would be out early, the time governed to a degree by the seasons of the year, walking and jogging on the roads for two to three hours to muscle up. Usually there would be a gallop, say, twice a week, but unlike most of the young horses, Mill House did not get a regular pop over the schooling fences. He was a natural jumper and like the established 'chasers needed little enough of that.

Back from exercise, it was a brush over, feet washed out, and then rugged up nice and warm, with water to drink and hay to munch while the lads set the boxes fair. And after the Head Lad had doled out the rations, the big horse like each of the others fed according to his own individual requirements, the hours were passed in quiet contentment until evening stables, starting around 4 pm. That brought, unfailingly, a visit from the trainer, the man on whose experience and skill, in the yard as well as on the gallops, rests much of the making or marring of a horse. He would be on his rounds for the second time that day to make sure that all was well, to feel legs, inquire which of his charges had eaten up and to ponder the problem of those that had not — a matter of importance, since on the verdict rests the amount of work to be prescribed.

Feeding is an art in itself, and some race-horses are unbelievably finicky, but Mill House has a big frame to fill and the appetite to go with it. He would happily clear up more than the fourteen to fifteen pounds of cracked oats mixed with chopped hay and a double handful of damp bran, considered a good ration for the average horse. And in addition he made no bones about finishing the daily two nets of hay with another at night for those that will eat it.

Racing days of course brought a change in the day-to-day routine, and on return from a meeting his lad would go over Mill House even more carefully than usual, looking for the tiny cuts and scratches that are, inevitably, part of life for a 'chaser. And if the horse had been jumping fences made up with furze that day then the inspection would be even more meticulous, because nothing festers quicker than a tiny gorse prickle, almost invisible and missed high inside the sufferer's flanks.

Once in England it was not long before Mill House was representing his adoptive country, carrying the flag against the Irish invader, the indomitable Arkle. Although the big horse appeared to be as Irish as his rival, bred by the Irish catering family, the Lawlors, out of Nas na Riogh, a little Irish mare they owned, and named after one of the Lawlor private homes, Mill House's sire was King Hal, and his grandparents on that side were Windsor Lad who won the Derby and St Ledger, and a mare Mary Tudor II, by the famous French but English-bred horse, Pharos, and there is nothing much more English than that. He was also to be the only horse in England or elsewhere that seemed to have the scope to measure up to Arkle. But before those mighty contests, and the speculation, the excitement, the stress and the tragedy to come, and while Arkle was flexing his limbs still safely on the other side of the Irish Sea, the big horse had a season to himself, and time afterwards to become established as one of the great.

That first season turned out to be a mixed bag, a foretaste of part of his career to come, one day with a brilliance that was breathtaking, the next with the carelessness, some whisper clumsiness, that could mar his efforts. He began with three outings over hurdles – his first race ending at the first flight where he fell. The next time out he was unplaced, too, but his jumping and the way he covered the ground caught the eye. At the third attempt he won – by one and a half lengths, showing the speed that was exciting in a four-year-old of his proportions.

There was to be no more time for hurdling after that, and Mill House was plunged straight into steeplechasing, if not at quite the deep end, then definitely not at the shallow. The chosen initiation was in the New Century Chase, a top-class race for novices at Hurst Park, and it proved an unfortunate beginning. The big horse made a bad mistake at Number Six, and without the time or opportunity a youngster needs to recover himself, complemented it with a crashing fall at the eighth.

That is not the best way of giving confidence to a novice 'chaser of any age, any more than Cheltenham, chosen for Mill House's next venture two months later, is the best nerve-restoring course for a shaken beginner. And after a hair-raising bungle at each of the first two fences there, Tim Bradshaw, the big horse's jockey that day, appreciated why his riding instructions laid more emphasis on getting round safely than on riding to win. Wisely he decided to concentrate on trying to restore the confidence in his own jumping that the big horse so blatantly lacked, and took him well wide of the other runners to receive what amounted to a 'school' over the fences. And much to the jockey's surprise, and gratification, without the distraction of other horses jumping close by, the treatment worked so well that Mill House began to jump better and better until, still pulling hard, he overhauled the leaders and won impressively by an easy two lengths.

That ended the 1961-2 season, and when the next began Mill House was in the experienced hands of Fulke Walwyn. By the time it ended he had chalked up four wins, including the Cheltenham Gold Cup, and one second place, in his five outings, and that record combined with his spectacular leaps over fences to boost him into star status. But although his jumping was phenomenal, it was not only the big horse's method of clearing fences that provided thrills for the crowds. Those that he hit produced an equally earth-shaking exhibition, and only his great strength and weight, and by then, supreme confidence, enabled him to surge on almost unchecked where another, inferior in physique or ability, must have been brought down.

On the outcome of that season Mill House deserved without doubt the greatness wished on him by his thousands of admirers, even though there were some who contended that he was too erratic to sustain his reputation. The sadness, from Mill House's point of view, was the same that dogged almost the span of his racing career – that in a season where he had four good wins out of five outings to his credit, the Irish challenger had run in seven races and won the lot. Pat Taaffe had been the one to visualise the big horse's destiny. When Mill House first went to Fulke Walwyn's yard, Pat wrote to his friend, G. Robinson, the stables' jockey, to tell him he would 'be up on the best horse in Britain . . . quite possibly in the world'.

But after Pat had discovered the truth for himself about the new young horse, Arkle, whom he also trained and rode, he wrote to his friend again: 'A correction, you are now up on the *second* best horse in the world'.

At the time, that was prophetic but unsubstantiated. Four of Arkle's races had been in Ireland, and after all, the mighty Mill House had taken his Gold Cup at Cheltenham by twelve lengths, and a month later the Mandarin Chase at Newbury with the power, and in the manner, that set people talking of a second Golden Miller. He was a proven champion, and apart from Arkle, as yet untested against him, in Mill House's day there was no horse to touch him.

At the beginning of the 1963-4 season the two met for the first time for the duel that had been the talking point with the racing fraternity for months, and that had also split the non-racing fraternity, the great, ordinary public hooked on 'chasing through the medium of TV, into two vociferous camps – Mill House or Arkle. They met on the 30 November, on a bleak, colourless day, in the Hennessy Gold Cup – and the big horse won.

That was the race where a slip, overjump, something, set Arkle back, and so Mill House won by eight lengths. Or so say the Arkleites. But the Mill House supporters, even those who concede that their great horse could never have matched Arkle in the time to come, contend that, slip or no, Arkle would not have been the victor that day – that he was the lesser horse, and it was in the succeeding three or four months when he shot ahead to outstrip the adjective 'great' and earn 'peerless', the one that stuck.

Whatever the truth, Mill House consolidated his triumph by taking the King George VI Chase in December and the Gainsborough Chase at Sandown in the following February. Less than a month later he and Arkle came up for the second round.

The big horse's trainer and enormous following of fans were confident – no question but that their fellow would trounce Arkle again – and so they remained for most of the way round in the Cheltenham Gold Cup of 1964. And even the top of the hill where the first real doubts were born, did not prepare them for the unbelievable, when Arkle sprinted after the last fence, and Mill House had already given, with a huge leap there, and had no more to offer. A second to Arkle there, another, when weighted down with 42 lb to Dormant in the Whitbread Gold Cup made a chastening finish to the season for the big horse.

Third round: 5 December 1964, the Hennessy Gold Cup at New-·bury. Mill House was rising eight and looked superb; he was receiving 3 lb from Arkle; of course he would make a come-back – who could doubt it? When the big horse really got going, when he made the prodigious jumps he could make and galloped as· he could gallop, there was no horse to stay with him. But that day there was Arkle, up alongside, matching each huge leap with one as splendid or better, galloping stride for stride until the pace and the pressure were too much and Mill House cracked. He finished fourth, dead weary and disheartened. Arkle won by twenty-eight lengths.

Some say the big horse was never the same again, and indeed, although he won the Mandarin Chase six weeks after the Hennessy defeat, it took every bit of the grit and courage of a superbly brave animal just to get his head in front to do it. But he took his next race, the Gainsborough Chase at Sandown, and he and Arkle came to the final round.

But no, the big horse was not the same – and the twenty lengths that left him trailing in second place were even more humiliating.

Training a big horse is never an easy job; the weight tells, and there is a bigger area where things can go wrong. For a while Mill House's forelegs had been suspect, he was never seen without bandages, but they held up in the autumn of 1965 long enough for him to boost his morale with a good second, and by winning a couple of easy races, the last at Cheltenham on 6 December. But the manner in which he had run to come third at Sandown in the Gallagher Gold Cup a month previously had not helped in the further confidence-restoring, and by March the next year he had broken down.

That could have been the end for Mill House, but there is little Fulke Walwyn does not know about 'bad legs', and they had the summer before them. And then, despite the odds against, another season to come.

To the spectators at the Massey Ferguson Gold Cup in December '66, it was a miracle of a come-back as the big horse fenced and galloped his way round with all the old gusto. And though one of his appalling mistakes at the open ditch there took all the punch out of him and he was unplaced, well, the two and a half miles were not far enough for him anyway. What mattered was that Mill House was back.

He was back, no doubt of that, and back in the public eye, cheered on by his delighted supporters when he followed up with a good third in the Great Yorkshire Chase, and then took the Gainsborough Chase for the third year running. And what he could not know was that by then Arkle, the unbeatable, was finished with racing forever.

So it was on to the Cheltenham Gold Cup, the race that no horse had ever won after a 'come-back', and even the most pessimistic were encouraged by the way the big horse performed at a school at Newbury ten days before.

But Mill House fell that day at Cheltenham, in his bid to win his second Gold Cup. From the start there was none of the usual battling to get at his fences, and when he was asked to stand back at the open ditch he failed to rise at all. And with that crash it seemed as though the big horse's luck had really run out, because in addition to his 'dickey' legs it was discovered he now had a back injury, supposedly a strained muscle.

A study of equine skeletons in the British Museum has shown that horses, like humans, are very prone to spinal trouble, even when young. And when Mill House eventually went to the Equine Research Station at Newmarket and was operated on, it was found that two of his vertebrae were fused together and had to be separated. Obviously if this condition had caused him a lot of discomfort Mill House could never have been the brilliant 'chaser he was, but a sudden twinge of pain could have been the cause of his occasional erratic jumping, even in the early days. And undoubtedly this was why that day at Cheltenham in 1967 he never took off at the open ditch, and went through the roots of the brush fence on the further side.

Nowadays this is why the big, brown, elderly gentleman just occasionally misses the odd stride, to the disquiet of his rider. In that short, sad season that ended the big horse's career in April 1968, it was again the sudden twinge that caused him to fall in his last two races. But before he finished with his racing days, Mill House had another fitting moment of glory.

He came to Sandown in the April before, and at ten years old and despite the not too dependable legs and back, took hold, 'pulling double', steaming into and over his fences with all the old verve and splendour. And if by the end of that three miles five furlongs he was more than tired and his jockey thought the finishing post would never come, Mill House won his Whitbread Gold Cup, and the £7,350 that went with it.

The crowds went mad, and the big horse forgot his weariness and cocked his ears and took the tribute as his right. As well he might, for this was the horse that thrilled all who saw him, whether in the flesh or on TV, with his superlative fencing and his great heart. He was a champion in his own sphere, and but for the misfortune of coinciding with Arkle, Mill House would have been the greatest of his time.

3
NIJINSKY

The Triple Crown is the supreme accolade of the flat-racing world, bestowed on the winner of all three of the greatest of the classic races, the Two Thousand Guineas, The Derby and the St Leger. It takes a very good horse to win just one of these races, and a great one to triumph in two. For a number of perfectly feasible reasons many exceptional animals never attempt the Triple Crown at all, but the fact remains that this award is the peak of an owner's ambition. And it takes a three-year-old of a versatility and eminence beyond the norm to win three very different types of race, varying in length from the mile of the Guineas up to the stamina-testing mile and a half of the Derby.

The first to do so was West Australian, in 1853, and then there were only a dozen winners until Bahram achieved the honour in 1935. After that came a long gap of thirty-five years, until the immortal Nijinsky galloped away with the distinction in 1970.

There was something special about Nijinsky right from the beginning. He was born in Canada, and although that country often produces fine race-horses, the blood-stock industry is a very small one compared with America and the climate far from ideal for breeding Thoroughbreds. Both his parents were also Canadian bred and owned by Mr Eddie Taylor, although Northern Dancer, Nijinsky's sire, made his racing name principally in the States and now stands, syndicated for $75,000 a share, at his owner's American stud at Chesapeake City.

Northern Dancer, a grand-son of the renowned Nearco, was a first foal and a very late one who never grew even as large as Hyperion, the famous pocket-sized 1933 Derby winner. He was an easy horse both to train and to race, and his illustrious son was to inherit both Northern Dancer's highly competetive spirit and his ability to finish very fast from any position his jockey chose to pick. Despite some foot trouble this horse was as thoroughly tested in his racing career as any horse could be, and emerged with flying colours. Amongst his many victories were the Kentucky Derby and the Preakness, races that constitute the first two legs of the American Triple Crown. In 1964 he was elected Canada's horse of the year, and in 1970 became World Champion Stallion, chiefly owing to the exploits of his brilliant son.

The pedigree, performance and conformation most likely to complement those of Northern Dancer were the factors that decreed that Flaming Page should be Nijinsky's dam. She was a big, rangy filly with a lot of quality, built like a true stayer and one of the best ever bred in Canada, but she was a late maturer, and only lightly raced, did not show her real form until nearly the end of her racing career. A nervous type that needed to be handled with care, Flaming Page was altogether very unlike the contented, compact little horse chosen for her mate.

Northern Dancer tends to sire two distinct types that appear alternately, either strong, 'flashy' chestnuts of the sprinter variety, or bays that are big, rangy racing-types like Nijinsky.

Nijinsky was born on 21 February at his breeder's Oshawa stud, where he and all the foals remained until the autumn when they were moved to Windfields Farm, Ontario. As a weanling he remained with the same bunch of foals, but as a yearling, like all the colts, he was given a two-acre paddock to himself. By then he was growing into a big, rugged colt, built more on the lines of his dam and with a nice disposition, but it was chiefly his good breeding and the length of his stride that made Eddie Taylor decide he would like to keep him. At the annual colt sales that year, therefore, Nijinsky was carrying the big off-putting reserve of $60,000, but it was still not enough. The price was sufficient to deter most would-be buyers but the late Mr Charles Engelhard, the American owner who achieved so much racing success on the eastern side of the Atlantic, eventually bought the horse for $84,000.

Like many Engelhard and other American horses, including his famous predecessor, Mr Raymond Guest's Sir Ivor, Nijinsky was sent to Ireland, to Ballydoyle, Vincent O'Brien's renowned training establishment in County Tipperary, considered by many to be the best in Europe. And here there was an added interest in Nijinsky because it was Vincent O'Brien, in Canada to report on another Eddie Brown horse, who saw him by chance and recommended that Mr Engelhard should buy him.

The colt was broken in that autumn and wintered well. So well in fact that by the spring he was distinctly above himself and could only be handled by two of Ballydoyle's finest horsemen. In their expert hands however he soon began to come to hand, and in April Liam Ward, the many-times Irish Champion Jockey who was always to partner the horse in Ireland, rode him for the first time. On that occasion Nijinsky did not prove a very easy ride, but Ward was definitely impressed, an effect that was strengthened as the colt settled with work and the jockey was able to ride him a few more times before partnering him in his first race, the Erne Stakes at The Curragh.

It was not a very important affair, six furlongs, £7 each with £800 added and 75 per cent to the winner, but Nijinsky dealt with it in the same way he was to treat his next two races. He won, very easily. And already his speed, particularly his inherited and fantastic acceleration, made it possible for Ward to drop him in behind horses at will, or pull him out and get going just when he pleased.

There had been no troubles since Nijinsky got over his 'spring fever', and he was proving the easiest of animals both at home and on the course. Unlike the majority of good horses the colt never 'took it easy' in his work at home. Where most would bother no more than to get their head in front of their working companion, whatever its standard, Nijinsky had the unusual trait of pricking his ears and galloping right away from other horses with obvious enjoyment. He never idled about on exercise, and was so active that he really needed comparatively little work and did best for being lightly trained. On the other hand he hated to be kept waiting around and showed it by playing up if he had to watch other horses working before it was his turn. His programme was therefore fitted to his special needs, and after exercising at walk and trot with other horses in the morning, he was kept apart with one other companion, walking around in a big barn until it was time to go on to the gallops. And on those stretches of good Irish turf it was soon made very plain that this horse was developing into something out of the ordinary.

On the race-course Nijinsky made no bother about such trifles as going into the starting stalls, he could have been ridden on the proverbial silken thread, and it made no difference which way the race was run: fast or slow, it came alike to this horse. The one question still to be answered was whether an animal of such exceptional speed could also be a stayer. And the reply was still not forthcoming after his third race, the Beresford Stakes, run over a mile in heavy going, where Nijinsky for the first time had to be shaken up a little to ensure a win by three-quarters of a length.

In October 1969, as his final effort as a two-year-old, Nijinsky came to England for the first time, to make a bid for the Dewhurst Stakes and the ten and a half thousand pound purse that went with the race. His reputation in Ireland preceded him, his jockey was Lester Piggott, and the opposition was moderate. Nijinsky started at 3–1, to win by three lengths on a tight rein.

Again the colt wintered well, again by spring he was feeling good, and, a bit of a handful, was still demanding the expert riding of the best lads in the yard. The Gladness Stakes at The Curragh, a good test of seven furlongs against horses of all ages, was his first engagement as a three-year-old, and during his preparation in March Lester Piggott came over and rode him. On the strength of that and without the ease of Nijinsky's forthcoming win – again in heavy going quite unsuited to his low, daisy-cutting action and when, according to Liam Ward, he was never at more than half-speed – Piggott made up his mind that the colt should be his mount for the Guineas. It was not long before the champion jockey decided that Nijinsky was the best of all the great horses he had ridden, an assessment he has never since altered or qualified.

To all who knew him, Nijinsky was by then as much of a certainty for the Guineas as any horse could be, but there were still doubts, at many levels, about his stamina for any race over the mile. After his victory in the Gladness his price was 9–4 for the Guineas, but only 8–1 for the Derby.

Vincent O'Brien had few doubts. He knew Nijinsky had the speed required for the Guineas, so set about training him for the one and a half miles of the Derby, teaching him to relax and conserve that speed so that he could get the extra distance as well.

On 27 April 1970 the horse came to Newmarket and won the Two Thousand Guineas by two and a half lengths, but there was no spectacular late run up the hill to thrill the crowds. Lester Piggott had been riding to orders. He was to let Nijinsky cruise along and go through the field without asking for any imposing, sudden acceleration that would light the horse up. He did just that and his mount did all that was required of him, but to some Nijinsky gave the impression that he was idling in front and that by the end of the race he had little left in reserve. In fact he had done an exceptionally fast time.

In the Derby parade of 1970 Nijinsky was sweating a little but looked what he was, massive, commanding, perhaps the most beautiful horse ever to be seen in a classic race the world over, and in performance a fantastic champion of champions. He went down to the start with Lester Piggott, ears pricked, moving beautifully, looking almost exactly the same as when he came to pass the starting post again as the winner. As the field swung round Tattenham Corner Nijinsky was just behind the three leaders, and up to the point where his jockey asked him to change gear he had once again just been cruising happily along. For a moment he paused as though surprised, then slipped into top, quickly passed the three horses in front, and proved himself one of the horses of the century by the effortless manner of his winning.

That made Nijinsky the fifth horse since the war to win the first two classics for colts. Ridden by Liam Ward he then added the Irish Derby for good measure – a race only twice achieved by an Epsom Derby winner – and with an impressive victory a month later, in the King George VI and Queen Elizabeth Stakes, ensured ten wins for

the ten outings of his racing career to date. With more than
£200,000 to his credit, he was already past the record in prize
money.

Nijinsky's programme included the Prix de l'Arc de Triomphe, run
in October and a most valuable and influential racing event, but at
that time there was no real thought of first running him in the St
Leger and so making a bid for the Triple Crown. And for all the lure
of that honour, and other considerations apart, it must always be
tempting, and often financially necessary, to let a great horse prove
his worth by doing just so much and then letting him earn it, at stud.
But there were telling articles by leading Sports Correspondents and
pleas from the public, and above all Mr Engelhard was first and fore-
most a true sportsman who liked to get fun out of his horses.

The decision was taken. Nijinsky should go for the St Leger
Stakes, but it was most unfortunate his preparation should then be
held up by a bad attack of American ring worm. He lost a lot of hair
round the saddle and girth area and could not be worked for a while,
and although apart from that the rash appeared to have no ill effect,
in retrospect Vincent O'Brien thinks the horse was not perhaps as
hard and fit as he should have been for a tough race over nearly a
mile and seven furlongs.

Whether this was a correct assessment or not made little difference
to the result of the St Leger, because Nijinsky won the race, and his
Triple Crown, with ears pricked and electrifying ease. But although
it was quickly regained, he did lose a lot of weight.

Maybe that was a pointer to his being a little below par; maybe it
was the pandemonium created by the hordes of photographers who
went mad the moment Nijinsky entered the parade ring at Long-
champs, and upset him; maybe it was partly the luck of a bad draw
in the line-up, or the fact that Lester Piggott did not ride the right
race for the horse on that day, on that course; maybe it was the little
swerve Nijinsky gave, away from the whip when nearly on the winning post, that was the deciding factor. More probably it was a combination of the lot, but sadly, what is still the greatest horse of the
century was beaten for the first time in the Arc de Triomphe, only by
a head by the French horse, Sassafras.

Even more sadly, Nijinsky then went for the mile and a quarter

Champion Stakes in which he was to redeem himself, and instead, in the last furlong, changing his legs and swishing his tail, proclaimed for all to see that he was not the horse he had been.

Two failures, but they could not diminish Nijinsky's stature, either on the race-course or ultimately at stud, for which he had already been syndicated for a record sum to stand in Kentucky. And his owner, whose opinion of his horse's true greatness, like that of Vincent O'Brien and Lester Piggott, never wavered, was the first to say that they had just asked too much, too often, of a young horse in a single year.

No horse could have been produced with better team-work by trainer, manager and jockey alike, and all the world wanted to see him retired undefeated. But if the decision to run in the St Leger was the one that robbed Nijinsky of this ultimate success, paradoxically it was also the one that gave him the supreme honour of joining the chosen few, the winners of the Triple Crown.

4

MANDARIN

There is no need of signposts to give you the vicinity, even the road signs depicting a horse are not necessary as a clue: you have only to note the behaviour of the traffic to tell you your destination is close by. For when lorries, motor-bikes, private cars or coaches alike not only slow down but often actually stop at first glimpse of a flesh and blood equine being ridden on or beside the road, then that untypical consideration spells racehorses and racehorse country – in this case, Lambourn.

It's Lambourn, too, in the chilly first light of a winter's morning, where the Guv'nor, Fulke Walwyn, is standing by the gate of his immaculately tidy yard, straining his eyes trying to pierce the misty gloom as he awaits the coming of his other string, from the additional establishment across the paddocks. They appear eventually *via* the road, the light clip-clopping of the hooves of a dozen or so young 'chasers preceding their arrival, walking in a deceptively decorous line, exercise sheets folded back at the corner, some with exercise bandages, mostly all wearing running-martingales, a few with the special rubber attachment that foils the tongue coming over the bit. Some of the lads have noses blue and pinched by the cold, and it's early but as they join the first string now filing out of the yard all of them are minutely attentive to what the Guv'nor has to say. For modes may alter in the world about, and the 'short back and sides' give way to, in this setting, curiously incongruous lengthy locks, but when it comes to manners and strict attention to the job in hand, with Fulke Walwyn nothing changes. Neither does he miss a trick. His eyes rove knowledgeably over each horse, maidens, recent winners, three-year-olds, the lot. 'You jog on, get up in front!' 'O.K. . . . you go on the roads . . . ' . 'You go this way – walk only!'

Up on the downs the light is struggling through but it's foggier and colder yet. The chill hits the horses, those that, led by a lop-eared veteran are to do seven furlongs on the public gallops, and there is the heady feel of good turf under their feet. As their lads walk them, twenty or so on a big circle round the trainer, the more exuberant, and that goes for most, take it in turns to explode in all directions like giant Chinese crackers at a fireworks party. Their riders, for all the apparent precariousness of the perched racing seat, remain literally unmoved and the Guv'nor looks pleased. His horses are feeling good.

More instructions. Some are to go one way, some another. There are orders about the pace. 'You lot . . . canter, but stop 'em well back coming down the hill . . . '. The two horses that are racing the next day go off, exclusive, with an old horse to lead them – and there is to be 'no just taking off any old how', they go in specific order and keep it.

The horses disappear. The chill bites, the wind wails but the fog only swirls and thickens. A curlew whistles, wild and high, there is the 'cheevick . . . cheevick . . . ' cry of partridge and a brace whirr up through the mist. Suddenly there's the rhythmic thudding of hooves, followed by the nebulous shapes of three horses cantering by, then a gap, then nine more looming through the murk with another three to follow. From out of the valley where the fog still lingers thick, an alien string appear. Up on the downs the fog is thinning, the sky lightens and the ghost of the sun attempts a break-through.

It's a scene, with variations in the weather conditions, that takes place 'chasing season after season with little change. It's a scene that became part of life to Mandarin, the little French-bred horse that arrived at Fulke Walwyn's yard in the summer of 1954. Only in his case the wind in his mane and the turf under his feet and the *joie de vivre* that has never left him, combined to make him so disruptive to general behaviour that he usually had to be isolated from the string, and sent off with only a relatively staid old-hand as pace-maker.

Many horses that subsequently become great at first give small hint of the triumphs to come, and with Mandarin this period of little promise seemed to be extended. As a young horse his physique did not help. He arrived at Lambourn on the fat side for a three-year-old, would-be racehorse, but once in training and starting to race he became irritatingly choosy, difficult to feed, and ran up very light. He was a small horse anyway, rich bay in colour, with an exceptionally high wither and a big 'jumping bump' topping strong quarters — all the best horses have the engine in the back. But as a four-year-old he was still angular, with little of the substance that came with maturity.

Time was to prove that Mandarin's biggest attribute as a jumper was his big heart, and in the years to come he was to win renown for his gameness in tackling fences. But at first jumping did not seem to be his *forte*, and apart from apparent speed and a certain look in his bold eye, that alert 'all there' expression of which old age has not robbed him, he seemed to possess few of the attributes of a hurdler, let alone a 'chaser.

It was not that Mandarin was unwilling to jump, but that due to the faulty methods of his initial part-breaking in he lacked the suppleness and consequent balance. After the horse arrived, Fulke Walwyn had tried everything he knew to remedy the situation, but Mandarin had already acquired the wooden mouth that made him resist the bit and jump stiff-backed off his forehand.

He did win his second race, but was unplaced in five of the nine outings of 1955–6. Of the remainder that season he scored twice when ridden by Fred Winter, one of the two jockeys that were to prove Mandarin's salvation. The first was a win at Sandown, where the little horse made all the running to prove that he could, after all, jump hurdles. The second established, with a third in a front-running, tough race over three miles, that Mandarin had the stamina and courage to match his speed and new jumping potential.

But hurdling is hurdling, and when it was then decided to try him 'chasing, it seemed to be courting disaster with a horse only just shedding a justified reputation as a bad jumper. That was where

Michael Scudamore, known for his skill with novice 'chasers, came in. He took on Mandarin's tuition over the sticks, and in 1956–7 riding the horse in all but two of his nine races, had three wins, one by twenty-five lengths in the Broadway Novices Chase, and four seconds, to their mutual credit. Mandarin ended that season with his first essay into really top-class company, by being only just beaten into second place in the Whitbread Gold Cup when ridden by the stable jockey, G. Madden. Mandarin had arrived, and although his looks still did not do justice to his stout heart, his 1957–8 season consolidated the fact.

In the Hennessy Gold Cup he took on horses like that hero from Scotland, The Callant, Much Obliged who won the Whitbread Gold Cup, and the first-class 'chaser Lochroe. When the race developed into a gruelling duel between the six-year-old Mandarin and Linwell – winner of the Cheltenham Gold Cup, who was conceding him 16lbs – the little horse rocketed up the hill to win by three lengths.

His distance was much nearer four miles than the three, run at corking speed over a sharp course, that constitute the King George VI Chase, yet he won it that season and was to repeat the effort two years later. He finished up in 1958 with a blunder that involved Linwell and left them both out in the cold in the Cheltenham Gold Cup; then with a win, gained with characteristic gutsy jumping and determination, in the Golden Miller Chase; and finally took another second in the Whitebread Gold Cup, the trophy that was always to elude him.

By this time Mandarin had earned himself a very special reputation with the racing fraternity, and in Fulke Walwyn's yard he had long been accorded the top place he has never relinquished. There, it is not only for his victories that they love him. His big heart and eagerness to tackle anything in the way of a fence have always held their admiration, but they cherish Mandarin also for himself. He was, and is, the little cocky character with the bold, bright eye, always kind in the stable and quiet to handle, and no trouble to catch when at grass, but very quick to seize any opportunity. When he was young you did not take chances about shutting his stable door or he would be out in a flash, taking a look round. Although on the day he managed it and they caught up with him two miles up the road, there was really little reason for anxiety – Mandarin is much too clever to come to harm. It was the same with training. He would never dream of kicking at another horse, but it could have been bad luck for 'Mush' Foster, who 'did' him and rode him at home, had he failed to sit tight or lost his concentration when riding Mandarin. The bay had an infinite repertoire with which to follow up the first light-hearted series of bucks, and he never galloped without putting his head on the floor and pulling like a train.

The public took the gallant little Mandarin to their hearts. They cheered him in his triumphs, and were thankful when a few month's rest immobilised in his box, healed the fibula in his hind leg fractured during the 1959 King George VI Chase in which he came third. They applauded him for the pluck he showed in so nearly pulling off his third attempt at the Whitbread Gold Cup, and again when only just beaten after some traumatic experiences with alien fences, during the Grand Steeplechase de Paris at Auteuil. But before the day that Mandarin turned a seemingly inevitable catastrophe into a victory that made racing history, there was to be luck, both good and bad, to be woven into the fabric of his racing career.

He was beaten first time out in his 1959–60 season, but with Fred Winter turned up trumps on the next occasion. Then he started favourite for the King George VI at Kempton, won it after a very hard race, and showed signs of tendon trouble soon after. That cut the season short, but his luck still held because Fulke Walwyn is a specialist in dealing with this kind of thing, and Mandarin was 'fired' and given a long rest before symptoms could become something more serious. But although sound again for the next season, the luck did not then run Mandarin's way.

He was now ten years old, and although he did notch up one win, and ran well to come third in the Cheltenham Gold Cup, he never really recovered from a bad fall early in the season. Despite that they made him and Fred Winter favourites for the 1960 Whitbread's, but once more Mandarin could not cope, and this time was unplaced.

There were many to think the little horse was finished, that he was now too old to have another day, but in the autumn of '61 he came out to win at Ludlow and then, looking as well and fit as ever in his life, took the Hennessy Gold Cup by a head. Snow precluded another go at the King George VI, but Mandarin, once again partnered by Fred Winter, was there to take on the field in the Cheltenham Gold Cup.

Fred Winter was another of the race riding artists who was as fine a horseman as he was jockey. As a rider he had the same understanding with his horses that has proved so successful as a trainer, and he and Mandarin got on exceptionally well together. Amongst other attributes were his strength of leg and drive and the fact that he understood more than many the real functions of the whip. He seldom used it to hit his horse, but had the expertise to gauge exactly the moment when it was really necessary. On that day at Cheltenham it was the couple of reminders that Mandarin received when they were 'getting nowhere' down the hill second time round, that shot him into first gear at just the right moment, and so gave him the accolade to his career so far, the most prized Gold Cup of all.

Up to and including that date in March 1962, Mandarin had been racing for eight seasons, had won eighteen of his fifty races, and had netted Madame Hennessy, his French owner, £29,773 in prize money.

The horse whose 'day was done' had won his last four races in a row, and that year he and Fred Winter came once more to Auteuil – *Dimanche 17 juin 1962 – Grand Steeplechase de Paris – (6.500 m) 25 obstacles*, and 250,000 francs as first prize. That was how the race-card had it.

The day was hot, too hot for comfort for riding in a National in France or anywhere else, but it was not sweat that was putting the sheen on Mandarin's bay coat as he pulled his jockey round the paddock. That was due to the same fine hard condition that made the muscles ripple over his quarters, and if the horse did not look all that impressive to the uninitiated, there was that unmistakable certain 'something' about him that still makes Mandarin stand out from the rest. He was moving beautifully as they went down to the start.

He passed the stands in front, pulling double and fighting for his head, the usual heavy-headed ride that had to be ridden in a rubber-covered snaffle to save damage to his mouth. The course is tortuous, turning and twisting, coming back again towards the stands after the first sharp left-handed bend, and as Mandarin went in to jump the big privet fence at Number Four, the metal chain inside that rubber bit snapped. It left Fred Winter with no contact with his horse's mouth, and no steerage except for the reins held together by the rings of an Irish martingale, the slender neck-strap attached to the breast-girth, and the limited guidance possible through shifting his body and balance. It left Mandarin, a hard-pulling 'chaser trained to gallop on the bit and used to the steady pressure of much of his jockey's weight counterpoised, through the reins, against his own mouth and forehand, to jump in a manner entirely foreign to him, with his head completely free.

So much for the dilemmas connected with the actual jumping of the twenty-one remaining fences, but there was a worse problem yet. Without steerage, how were they to find their way at racing speed over a course, set more or less in a design of two figures of eight going in opposite directions, where some of the bends go through an angle of 180° and there is then an entire circuit to be made round the out-side for good measure?

The French jockeys helped, edging Mandarin round some of the bends with admirable sportsmanship, in a situation where it would have been so easy, and so tempting, to 'help' him to run off course; Fred Winter's outstanding strength of leg and grip drove Mandarin on where needed, and somehow served to bring him round in that agonising moment when the little horse started to make for a fence jumped first time round. In the earlier stages it was a big help not to be quite out in front alone but basically it was the fantastic riding of a past master at the game, combined with a courageous horse's own innate good racing sense that kept him from trying to run away when there was no braking system to check him, and his indomitable heart that kept them going when no-one watching believed it possible. Somehow Mandarin kept on his feet when he so nearly made a disas-ter of the 'Rivière de la Tribune' in front of the stands; somehow they got back to the correct track when he hesitated at the last right-handed bend where it was as simple to go two ways, both wrong, as the right one. Even so that moment of indecision lost them precious ground, and as they faced the Bullfinch and the welcome last straight, they were lying fifth.

When people first realised what had happened and that Mandarin was virtually rudderless, their reaction had been the fervent prayer that there would not be an accident; then, as horse and jockey miraculously continued to survive, it seemed that they might actually get round the course. Now, over those last fences as Winter went into over-drive, as Mandarin, deadly tired, the suspect tendon in his foreleg already given way, responded in the manner he always had and battling, head outstretched, passed three horses in 100 yards to take the lead, the impossibility was there . . . now it was, *could* Mandarin win?

The long run-in seemed as though it would never end and inch by inch Lumino, one of the French horses, was overhauling him. At the post no-one could tell, it was as close as that, but as Mandarin came in dead-beat, sweat-streaked, so tired he almost fell, the numbers went up in the frame to prove that miracles can happen – and the reception he and his jockey received almost did justice to a racing event that will probably never be equalled.

Mandarin had indeed broken down in the later stages of the race, but anyway they had always said they would retire him if he won that year at Auteuil. He came back to Lambourn, a hero amongst heroes, to take as his due the affection of all those who have contact with him, and the admiration of all those members of the public who still come to pay homage. In old age Mandarin is still cock of the walk in Fulke Walwyn's yard, his eye as bright, his interest in all that goes on as undiminished as in his racing days. When his trainer thought to use him as a hack on the gallops, Mandarin displayed an unabated determination to go with the string, and no less vigour in the fireworks he put on when this was discouraged. For a long time now it has, perforce, appeared more prudent to allow the little horse to take his exercise decorously led out in hand around the lanes, or in a paddock in the company of some unbroken youngster. And when, a few years back, he visited Cheltenham, the scene of some of his greatest triumphs, in a parade before the Hennessy Gold Cup in company with his famous stable-mates, Mill House and Taxidermist, it was difficult to say which of the sprightly veterans enjoyed it most, which was the most eager and ready to be off.

5

MILL REEF

No-one at Ian Balding's training stables at Kingsclere, Berkshire, will ever forget a certain day in August 1972. It started much as any other day at that admirably run establishment, where around seventy at a time of the most blue-blooded and valuable throughbred colts and fillies in the world are trained, and sent about their mission in life – top class racing on the flat, or over hurdles. There were horses going out on exercise, a couple of youngsters, tacked up in roller and crupper, being lunged in the circular school, and here and there a stable lad was sweeping the already scrupulously clean yards.

Up on the downs, on the very best of the training ground, some of the older horses were at work under the searching eyes of Ian Balding, who was riding The Brigand, the ex-point-to-pointer that he uses as a trainer's hack. As always he was giving meticulous attention to each animal in turn but his mind was particularly occupied with Mill Reef, the incredible little super horse, the 'one in a million' whose programme had been interrupted of late by a spell of the ill luck that dogs most racehorses at some time or another. Now things were coming right once more, and this was the horse's third period of work since his last enforced rest. There was nothing very strenuous about it, just a nice strong canter over seven furlongs.

The going was firm, but then all ground came alike to this horse, and Balding noted how well he was going as he passed, swinging along following Merry Slipper, the lead horse, at a steady pace over the remaining furlong.

For a moment the trainer turned away to watch the next pair coming up, and when he looked again his heart missed a beat. Mill Reef was off the gallop, standing to one side, with John Hallum, the lad who looked after him from the day of his arrival at Kingsclere, down out of the saddle and holding one of the horse's forelegs.

Clearly there was something very wrong, but as the trainer switched The Brigand round and cantered towards them, the worst disaster that crossed his mind was that Mill Reef could have split a pastern, a common injury and relatively serious – it can put an end to a horse's racing career, for instance – but one that has, anyway, no effect on its potential at stud. But as he jumped off The Brigand to see John Hallum's ashen face and shaking hands, and took in the ominous words: 'I heard a horrible crack . . . '. Balding realised that this was something very much more calamitous. When John added that he had been unable to pull Mill Reef up afterwards for all of 100 yards, the trainer knew too that any initial damage must have been exaggerated.

Mill Reef belongs to Mr Paul Mellon, an American, and was foaled at his lovely Rokeby Farm in Virginia, about fifty miles from Washington. The horse was sired by Never Bend, one of Nasrullah's best sons who came second in the one and a quarter mile Kentucky Derby. Both his dam, Milan Mill, and his grand-dam were bred at Rokeby, and his female line includes Black Ray, the little 'bargain' mare bought by Captain Sir Cecil Boyd-Rochford in 1922, that afterwards bred nine winners in England and one in America. Like all American Thoroughbreds Mill Reef was backed at a very early age, and when he arrived at Kingsclere, as a yearling in October 1969, he was already broken in.

The American 'Mellon' colts are nearly always the nicest of all those that come to Kingsclere, and their advent is eagerly awaited. In that particular draft there were two that stood out above the rest, a well grown, big, quality colt – later to be named Quantico – by the great American sire Graustark, and this other, equally well bred, that was beautifully proportioned but very much smaller. At first sight it was the larger animal that caught the eye, but the moment they were cantered the small colt's graceful action seemed to place him in a class by himself. Yet as all trainers know the most beautiful action in a young animal can be misleading, many additional qualities go to the making of an outstanding racehorse, and numerous yearlings that are lovely movers at the canter do not prove to be really fast when it comes to galloping. So that Ian Balding's first impression of Mill Reef was that here was another attractive, typically mature if small, American yearling, that moved unusually well and should turn into a really nice two-year-old. But there are so many good ones arriving at that establishment that never in his wildest dreams did he visualise the small colt turning out to be one of the great mile and a half horses of all time.

Mill Reef proved to be an exceptional two-year-old. He had developed into a lovely looking small thoroughbred, black points (that is 'stockings', mane and tail) setting off his rich bay colouring, a neat head, courageous, kind eye, and a temperament to match his elegance. He ran six times during that season in England, achieving the grand slam by winning all four of the top two-year-old races – the Coventry Stakes at Ascot, the Gimcrack at York, the Imperial Stakes at Kempton, and finally the Dewhurst at Newmarket. Three of them were very easy wins, he took the Gimcrack by ten lengths in heavy going, and the only anxious moment was at Kempton, when he just got up to the good filly Hecla to beat her by a length. In France, after travelling badly and with a bad draw, Mill Reef himself went under in the Prix Robert Papin, beaten by a short head by another outstanding two-year-old, My Swallow, who won the French grand-slam.

By the end of that season Mill Reef had won more prize money in England than any horse of his age before. He was obviously an outstanding animal and looked to be an exceptional candidate for, at any rate, the 1971 Two Thousand Guineas. But not even Ian Balding thought that Mill Reef would stay more than a mile, which is the length of that race. By his breeding he was not bound to be a stayer, and this was emphasised by his apparently headstrong style of racing, winning most of his races from start to finish which is not normally the way to get a mile and a quarter, and more usually denotes a sprinter.

As a three-year-old Mill Reef started with the Greenham Stakes at Newbury with an effortless win, and far and away the best public trial by any of the contenders for the Two Thousand Guineas. The race was only seven furlongs – and the Derby is five furlongs further – but that was when the horse's jockey, Geoff Lewis, proved his own good judgement by making a prophecy. He said that right from the start of the race his horse had given him the feeling that even if they did not win the Guineas, he would guarantee they would win the Derby – a complete reversal of what most people considered to be Mill Reef's capabilities.

Three weeks later the colt went to Newmarket to face the smallest but most select Guineas' field for years. With only six starters, Mill Reef was favourite, My Swallow second favourite, and the legendary Brigadier Gerard, who had not had a previous race that season, as third favourite. And the Brigadier won, and won well, by three lengths and still going away. There are many theories about this result. If one goes by the saying that 'a good big 'un will beat a good little 'un', then the Brigadier, grown into a majestic three-year-old, a size bigger all round than Mill Reef's lovely 15 hands 3 inches. proportions, had the edge. But like most adages that one is frequently discounted, and even though according to the form book: 'Brigadier Gerard – looked well, led over one furlong out, ran on well, won by three lengths. Mill Reef . . . hard ridden, unable to quicken', it *still* does not quite add up.

No-one could deny that Brigadier Gerard is a great horse and a truly great miler, who outdid both Mill Reef and My Swallow on that day for speed. But though Balding would not have wished his horse to take on the Brigadier again . . . *over a mile* . . . and was terribly disappointed, he does not consider he was wrong at the time in his conviction that Mill Reef had an outstanding chance. Many think the race was run too slowly overall for the smaller horse to wear down his opponents in the manner that usually proved so successful, and maybe his and My Swallow's jockeys were so concerned with each other's tactics that they overlooked Joe Mercer and the Brigadier, tucked in behind and able to come with a devastating swoop to beat them both.

But whatever the shortcomings in the Guineas, on Derby Day the little bay horse more than justified his supporter's faith in him. He did not run between these two big contests, but had been given one good gallop over a mile and a quarter up on the downs near home. Horses are not machines and there can be complex, sometimes very human reasons for their running better on one day than on another. Nor, as with athletes is it easy to bring a racehorse to the required peak of fitness and keep him there, or let him down a little and bring him again for the specified occasion. Certainly Mill Reef looked in even better condition on Derby Day 1971, his coat gleaming over the rippling muscles, and very much 'on his toes' as he always was, with the good racehorse's full awareness of his own, and the day's importance.

The opposition was strong, but Mill Reef, looking the winner right from the start, gave Geoff Lewis a beautiful ride. Always well and handily placed, when asked he came on with a lovely turn of foot to stay on well and win by two and a half lengths. Linden Tree, wearing blinkers for the first time and making all the running, ran a terrific race to be second; Irish Ball, later a comfortable winner of the Irish Derby, was third; Homeric fourth, and Athens Wood, who won the St Ledger that year, fifth.

It was a more than satisfactory performance, and afterwards Mill Reef continued to improve right to the end of the season. Owner and trainer resisted the temptation to run their horse in the Irish Derby and instead he took on the older horses for the first time in the Eclipse Stakes at Sandown. By now Mill Reef had a pace-maker, a horse called Bright Beam specially bought for the job, and he set a cracking pace. The main dangers were Welsh Pageant, at the time the best older English miler, and Caro, a very good horse indeed from across the Channel. But the strong opposition and the fact that they were older animals were not the only difficulties to be faced. The chief hazard was going back to a mile and a quarter race, after winning the mile and a half Derby. Amongst other technicalities it means quickening at a different point in the race, and it is perhaps unusual after training a horse for the longer distance to bring him back to the shorter, but it made little difference to Mill Reef. He and the French

Caro virtually had the race to themselves, and coming to the last three furlongs Mill Reef strode away to win by an impressive four lengths, breaking the course record. Three weeks later he was back to a mile and a half again for the King George VI and Queen Elizabeth Stakes, once more taking on all the best middle-distance three-year-olds with the exception of Linden Tree. He trounced the lot at a speed that from the start totally defeated the use of his pace-maker, and gave him an almost derisively easy win of six lengths.

For a long time it had been obvious that the British turf was harbouring two racing giants. Both Mill Reef and Brigadier Gerard were champions in their own right, both had caught the popular imagination, and each, the superbly elegant little horse and his imposing rival, had a huge following. When would they meet? And what would be the outcome? And the relief and excitement mounted when it was known that Mr Mellon, Mill Reef's owner, and Mr and Mrs John Hislop who bred and possess Brigadier Gerard, had decided to let their brilliant horses remain in training as four-year-olds: the duel would surely come the following year.

In the meantime, as a wind up to his great season as a three-year-old, Mill Reef went again to France. The Prix de L'Arc de Triomphe is a race for connoisseurs, a plum that tempts the cream of the past seasons, the winners and near winners of the Classics. It is run at Longchamp, between the huge network of grandstands and balconies, in October, when red and gold tinting the green of the trees adds to the attractions of the setting.

Up till then Mill Reef had had a tough season, and with no suitable preparatory race for this one, and the knowledge that he had anyway another season of racing in which to add to his laurels, he had been given a well-deserved rest. Possibly by the time of the race he was in fact past his peak. He had put on a public gallop at Newbury, which pleased those of his followers who were able to get there, as well as his trainer, but it is never easy to ensure that a horse is one hundred per cent fit after so long a spell off the course. Despite this, Geoff Lewis had a superb ride and Mill Reef achieved what Ian Balding considers his most thrilling performance, finishing another wonderful year by winning this much prized French race, in the fastest time ever.

The programme mapped out for Mr Mellon's horse as a four-year-old was to start with a preliminary spin at Newbury, followed by a 'go' for the very valuable Prix Ganay in France. The Coronation Cup would come five weeks later and four weeks after that, the Eclipse.

There had been no pre-arranged plan to ensure a meeting between Mill Reef and Brigadier Gerard, but both owners and trainers were content to leave it to the luck of the draw – and if the two horses met, they met. As it happened the Eclipse Stakes at Sandown were obviously on the racing programmes of both animals, and so everyone concerned as well as the racing public could look forward with mounting excitement to the battle of the giants.

Ian Balding was confident of the result. The Eclipse is for three- and four-year-old horses and is run over one and a quarter miles, a good length for Mill Reef, and one that favoured his style of racing more than that of the Brigadier, at his best over a mile. The smaller horse now had two pace-makers to ensure the strong, early pace he needed. He had proved himself a super horse in all conditions and at all distances, but he always pulled hard and a real speed from the start enabled Geoff Lewis to settle his horse, while taking the edge off the others. Mill Reef's great strength and superiority lay in his ability to keep up this tremendously strong gallop, and when the others began to flounder over the last couple of furlongs the small horse just swept remorselessly on, and on, and on . . . .

The policy paid off handsomely in the Prix Ganay. Except for Pistol Packer, sadly absent through an accident, all the best mile and a quarter horses in France were out to head the English contender. On the day his lead horse, this time Merry Slipper, made a very fast gallop, but as they turned into the straight Lewis let Mill Reef go on and he sailed home by an incredible ten lengths.

During the ensuing lapse before the Coronation Cup he was given a two weeks' easy, and when he started work again in a three week build up before the race, his response, or lack of it was puzzling. There was nothing one could pin-point exactly, no symptoms of ill-health, but he blew exceptionally hard and somehow seemed to lack the sparkle that one always connected with Mill Reef. It seemed he must have been given too long a time off, he was, perhaps, a little gross, and he was given a lot of extra work — too much in too short a time as good preparation for the race, as his trainer knew, but it did not look as though the opposition amounted to much.

There were only four runners with Homeric, the most serious rival, a good, tough horse but not apparently in the same class. As usual Bright Beam ensured the pace and as normal Mill Reef came up to Homeric about two furlongs from home, but that was almost all. Just at the moment when he could be expected to come shooting by he faltered, laboured, and hung on. Lewis had to pull his whip through, not to use it but to wave it at the little horse to ensure they won the race. And win they did, by a neck, and it could have been considered a clever win, judged to a hair's breadth without making a hard race of it, but everyone who really knew him realised that this was not the Mill Reef they had come to expect.

At that same meeting the normally consistent Martinmass, another Kingsclere horse, ran appallingly badly, and when two or three others from the yard did the same thing at about the same time, it was obvious that the dreaded virus affecting the top of the nose, an infection called rhinoneumanitis that had been sweeping other training establishments, was with them. Yet still no one suspected that Mill Reef had already been suffering from the complaint and had been trained for, and run, in the Coronation Cup while he had it — because he had shown no definite symptoms of any sort, not even the slightest rise in temperature. There was great anxiety in case he should be the next to catch the bug, and so miss the Eclipse Stakes and his appointment with Brigadier Gerard. Then two weeks before the big race Mill Reef did run a temperature one night. As it happened it was only a temporary set-back, but combined with his inexplicable lacklustre performance in the Cup it seemed odds on he had the infection, and he was scratched from the Eclipse. A decision that relieved Ian Balding at the time — because Brigadier Gerard is no horse to take on unless one's own animal is 'at the peak' — and even more when he eventually realised that Mill Reef had indeed had rhinoneumanitis, an illness from which it takes a long while to recover.

In fact he could not be got right in time for the King George VI and Queen Elizabeth Stakes towards the end of July, and that, as the main summer objective, was an even greater disappointment. So Mill Reef was given a rest and it was hoped to get him fit for the Benson and Hedges race at York a month later, which looked like producing the eagerly awaited meeting with Brigadier Gerard. But once again ill luck stepped in.

A shoe was lost during a training spin, the kind of little mishap that could and does happen a hundred times with no ill effect, but Mill Reef managed to give himself a little knock on his near fore that took a while to come right, and just as it did he pulled a muscle in his hindquarter. So that put paid to any aspirations to race in York. There was now only the Arc de Triomphe left, with the chance still there to double up on the success of the previous year – but Mill Reef never got to Longchamp in 1972. He was never to appear on a race-course again, because he broke his leg.

As well as looking after Mill Reef, John Hallum usually rode him at exercise and found him 'terrific', a stable lad's dream, always going on twice as well as any other horse. But in addition to the ride he gave you the horse was such a charming character to care for, in his ways more like a pony than a temperamental blood stallion. He had his fun, whipping round each time he passed the door of the indoor school when exercising at the trot there in the winter was one of his jokes, but he never bucked or kicked and there was not a shred of vice in him. Above all Mill Reef has always been a contented, happy little horse, taking life as he finds it with the minimum of fuss and the maximum of intelligence – two virtues that were to stand him in particularly good stead.

After the accident on that fateful day on the gallops, there were twenty minutes or so to wait for the horse-box to arrive, but Mill Reef seemed quite unworried. They had taken his saddle off and put on another exercise sheet for warmth, and though he made no attempt to put any weight on his near fore-leg, he seemed quite content to stand around picking at the grass. It proved impossible to get the box right on to the gallops, although where they parked there was a convenient little dip that lessened the steep angle of the ramp. But first there was all of twenty-five yards to go on the level – and that took another twenty minutes at least. For Mill Reef did not know how to walk on three legs, and by the time they had negotiated the short distance to the edge of the ramp, everyone was wondering how on earth they were going to get him up into the box. And there's no lifting up or pushing up a blood stallion with only three usable legs, if he does not want to go. But Mill Reef cocked his ears and considered the situation, and it was as if he knew there was no other way for suddenly, just on his own, he took two big, three-legged strides and he was up and in. It was a brave and brainy thing to do, but then the pain started, the first he had felt, and though they drove down as slowly as possible he was soaked in sweat by the time they got back to the yard.

Now there was the problem of how to get him out, but once more he solved the difficulty of his own accord and hobbled down the unloading ramp and round to his box.

The usual vet, Peter Scott Dunn, was away at Munich in charge of the Olympic horses, but his assistant gave a pain killer and tried to assess the damage. The main break was in front, at the bottom of the cannon bone, and that was bad enough, but the feel of the back of the fetlock joint was terrible, like a little bag of marbles.

The X-rays confirmed the vet's forebodings, but once the leg was plastered – a proceeding that Mill Reef took with quiet interest – he appeared quite unconcerned. Pain-killers were only necessary for the first two days, he always finished up the relatively small amount of food that could be allowed, and since the plaster was only to the knee he was able to get down and up again. Neither then nor at any other time did the little horse seem to be feeling sorry for himself.

There was no difficulty about meeting the cost of all that had to be done and obviously no expense was spared, but although no-one could or would minimise the incalculable monetary loss if such a horse should be lost to stud, this was never the only, or even the first consideration. All along the deep anxiety of everyone concerned was most plainly for Mill Reef himself, the personality all at Kingsclere had loved and cared for and been so proud of from the moment he arrived at the yard. Three of the best vets in the world came to consult on what could be done, and the operation, performed by Jim Roberts the eminent horse surgeon, took place a week later. It was none too soon, for although the bone had not perforated the skin, X-rays showed that the break was growing worse.

A 'theatre' was fixed up at one end of the big building that had just been re-furbished as a staff gymnasium, with tables for the surgeon's tools and the oxygen apparatus, and the Head Lad's bathroom, *via* a communicating door, commandeered as a dark room for developing X-rays on the spot. Straw bales covered with cellophane sheets barricaded off the required space, and Mill Reef stood against more bales, placed three high to form a 'table'.

He was in his own surroundings amongst people he knew and trusted, and he remained totally calm and relaxed – so much so that during the eight hours he was 'out', the anaesthetic, (and for a horse that is the most dangerous part of an operation), contained only two per cent of Fluothane mixed with oxygen, instead of the customary four per cent.

Fifteen minutes after a tranquilliser had been administered, the actual 'knock out' was fed into Mill Reef's jugular vein. And at the precise moment he was about to collapse into unconsciousness, the surgeon said 'Now!' and by hauling on the ropes round neck, girth and tail, the horse was pulled, without a sign of a struggle, onto the improvised operating table.

Everything went according to plan, and when the seven-hour operation was over they slid the patient down onto a thick straw bed and waited for him to come round. This is the moment when horses normally struggle, the reaction usually greater with colts than with fillies, but this horse made one little abortive attempt to get up and then, after a few minutes thought, tried again successfully, to stand quietly accepting everything including the new plaster that went right up to his elbow.

They kept a round-the-clock watch on him for the first crucial twenty-four hours, and the only problem was that he could not work out how to lie down with one stiff leg, and refused to be helped. But the first moment he was left alone Mill Reef devised a method, by leaning against the surrounding straw bales, the plastered leg stuck out straight, and sliding himself gently down on to his bed.

The plaster stayed on for the next six weeks and the patient learned to cope quite well, and liked being led round the yard for exercise. The troubles started when the plaster was replaced with a felt support. At once Mill Reef's confidence ebbed, he would put no weight on the injured leg and used only the toe so that the shoulder muscles on that side were wasting, and the back of the joints were not getting the exercise that was essential. With hind legs slipping under him, it was a horrible effort to move him fifty yards in ten minutes, and clearly something had to be done.

They taught the little horse to walk again with the aid of a length of string, attached to his fetlock joint and pulled each time the injured leg was about to move forward. A false 'heel', that was gradually lowered, eased the process and from the moment he was shod – no simple task as he had to be 'man-handled' to make him stand on the bad leg – Mill Reef never looked back.

During the good weather he went each afternoon into the grass enclosure within the circular exercise track, a place he always loved, where he could nibble the grass, have a little trot, and a roll in the sand-pit. By December that year he was exercising daily on the covered track at a kind of 'hobbly' hand canter, with John Hallum, perforce a very fit man, jogging beside him and a boy running behind to keep him going. Seen for the first time the horse still appeared very lame, but to his trainer and devoted lad the improvement was a miracle. By then he was in fact in no pain at all and when his attention was distracted from the injury, he was as near sound as a slightly lengthened leg and superficially less flexible joint seemed ever likely to allow.

The build up of exercise in the past four weeks had made it possible to increase his food, to vary it from the invalid diet of hay and mash to more fattening and muscle making protein, of great importance if he was to go to stud in the spring of '73. An electrical impulse machine that exercises the muscles was the one form of treatment that Mill Reef refused to tolerate, but hand massage and wisping were gradually bringing him into condition and his coat began to show a lovely bloom. He was still living in the spacious 'gymnasium', the floor room increased by moving back the retaining straw bales so that he could rest or mooch around as he liked, and the walls decorated with the letters, telegrams and get-well cards from his hundreds of admirers. Mill Reef has always enjoyed meeting his 'fans'. When he came home after winning the Derby the whole village turned out to greet him, watching him unload and, as he was allowed a pick of grass, pressing round to pat him and pull souvenir hairs from his tail, to his obvious unconcern and content. During the racing season he used to hold court in the circular ride, usually when there was a cricket match on anyway, and loved to be photographed and petted. In the early days after his accident he did get a little bit cheeky when his door was open and he could expect a sugar nob or piece of carrot or just a handful of grass from everyone at the yard who passed.

It was early in December, too, that Mill Reef appeared on television, treating strange producers, cameramen and all the paraphernalia that goes with them, with the same happy co-operation with which he accepts a peppermint!

In January 1973 Mill Reef left Kingsclere, and 600 people turned up on the Sunday before to give him a send-off. Now he is happily ensconced in the beautiful surroundings of the National Stud, in the company of such great stallions as Never Say Die and Hopeful Venture, and where the public who normally visit the Stud to the tune of 20,000 a year, will be able to see him – to his and their mutual satisfaction. He looks marvellous, is walking ninety nine per cent sound and has now made virtually a complete recovery.

Mill Reef successfully began his stud duties in March that year, and was limited to twenty-three mares in his first season. Six nominations were offered to the National Stud and made available by ballot to British breeders. And at around £10,000 a nomination, his record £300,414 in prize money could well be boosted to life earnings around the three and a half million mark.

Whether Mill Reef will remain at the National Stud or whether his owner will want him back in America, is a matter for the future. But either way he may well include Example, the Queen's outstanding filly, amongst his future wives. And if that occurs the progeny of such a match could well be another champion amongst champions. It could also add a nice touch of romance to the story of Mill Reef's life to date – another version of 'boy meets girl' – for when Mill Reef and Example were yearlings at Kingsclere, they used to go out on exercise together!

6
BRIGADIER GERARD

To own a horse at all is a very worthwhile experience; to own a horse that proves a winner within its own particular sphere, is an eminently satisfactory one; to breed a horse according to one's own scientifically formulated ideas, to watch it grow into faultless beauty, and then to have it triumph in every test of a carefully planned career, is something that occurs only to the chosen few. But it did happen to John and Jean Hislop, and the horse concerned is called Brigadier Gerard.

Compared with that of the late Lord Astor the Hislop stud is very small indeed, but in both cases the principles for breeding racehorses are, deliberately, much the same and based on a scientific approach. To some extent anyone who attempts to breed fine pedigree animals has to study heredity, but this particular system goes much deeper than that. It involves the minute tabulating of the good and bad points of each mare, and those of her ancestors for many generations back and then, by using the same method, discovering which stallion would be most likely to compensate for the dam's defects in any resulting progeny. In Lord Astor's case this produced less winners than other breeders of his time, but gave him the best overall proportion of results for the number of brood mares. And when the Hislops eventually set up on their own they adopted the same idea, scaled down to fit within their limits.

John Hislop had always wanted to breed racehorses, but could not find the means until after the Second World War. He managed it then by forming a partnership that was made viable by selling the products as yearlings and by buying and selling other horses as well — with his own share of the enterprise boosted with his earnings as a Racing Correspondent. This continued for some years and was fine, but he still nursed two unfulfilled ambitions.

The first, and the first to be achieved, was to possess a horse descended from the wonderful racing mare Pretty Polly, in 1904 the winner of the One Thousand Guineas, the Oaks and the St Leger, an animal whose long dead presence and famous blood had dominated the training stable and horses where John worked and rode as a young man.

When the opportunity arose, the accomplishment of his second aspiration, to acquire his own stud where he could concentrate on scientific selective breeding and race the results instead of selling them, involved his wife's whole-hearted co-operation and mutual monetary risk. It also meant the financial necessity of parting with all the brood mares bar two. Fortunately one of these was the last foal of Brazen Molly, the supposedly barren mare bought cheap for £400 in 1945, that as a great-grand-daughter of Pretty Polly had given the Hislops their link with that legendary animal. Under Hislop management Brazen Molly had then refuted her reputed sterility and already provided them with several useful offspring, even before the advent of La Paiva, her final fling and, as it turned out, her masterpiece.

Before blindness in one eye precluded La Paiva from the racecourse she had been placed on several occasions, but it was her exceptional looks combined with her Pretty Polly blood, rather than her prowess as a racehorse, that made the filly such an obvious choice for scientific breeding. Her only drawback was that the Pretty Polly inheritance also gave her the tendency to transmit to later generations the bony enlargements on hocks called curbs, from which neither she nor her own foals suffered but which sometimes appeared in her grandchildren. The problem was therefore to find a stallion without a trace of this trend in his pedigree, and since cost was also a major limiting factor, the search was not an easy one.

The very high stud fees demanded for sires likely to breed animals of both speed and the staying power to cope with classic races of much more than a mile, narrowed their quest to the field of possible 'milers'. Eventually the choice fell on Queen's Hussar, an admirably proportioned but then 'unfashionable' stallion at a reasonable price, who, had his racing career demanded it could have been a classic miler and who bore a striking resemblance to Fairway, the illustrious ancestor who figures prominently in his pedigree.

With two handsome parents and both Pretty Polly and Fairway blood in his veins, it was not altogether surprising that even at a few days old La Paiva's colt foal had a 'presence' that made him stand out on his own. They called him Brigadier Gerard — and since the dashing, fictitious French Officer of that name was a Hussar, the choice was a subtle one — and because the Hislop stud is too small to provide indoor coverage all the year, this colt like all the young stock, spent a lot of time outside. A first-hand acquaintance with all but the worst of weather combined with good management, makes for hardiness, and by the time Brigadier Gerard was a yearling he was already strong and well-grown and possessed of the robust constitution that has stood him so well. He was also already learning his trade with the trainer Dick Hearn, and it was while his owners were watching their colt at work with two-year-olds, where his long-striding canter was matching up to his work-mates' gallop, that the Hislops first realised just what a potentially really great horse they had succeeded in breeding.

If the fact needed any confirmation, Brigadier Gerard's owners received it at the end of his first racing season, after he had won the Middle Park Stakes, a top race for two-year-olds. On that occasion they were offered, and refused, £250,000 for their horse. As a four-year-old winner of thirteen races, the Hislops reckon they could have sold him in America for any sum they cared to name, but the Brigadier was not for sale, at home or abroad, either then or later.

He ended up by winning fifteen of his sixteen races, for a total of £203,213. His victories included the Two Thousand Guineas as a three-year-old, and in 1972 the Eclipse Stakes. And that year also saw the most famous of all, an achievement seldom equalled by any horse in the world, when, of then unproved stamina and attempting a mile and a half for the first time, he won the King George VI and Queen Elizabeth Stakes, from representatives of very nearly all the best in European racing.

The programme mapped out for Brigadier Gerard's racing career was in many ways as unconventional as his breeding, but was based almost entirely on what by ancestry he should be expected to achieve, and then extended to the distances his courage made possible. As a three-year-old he did not go for the Derby, because he was not bred for it. He did not race in France, where much of the racing money lies, because that would have interfered with his prescribed schedule. He was never over-raced. He had no preparatory race at all before the Two Thousand Guineas, because his owners and trainer felt it would be ideal, if it were possible to get him fit without, to let him come straight to the big race – and his trainer had the skill to do it. And if owners and trainer had had ideas of giving Brigadier Gerard more races than planned, the horse himself made it plain that it would not be a good idea.

A large proportion of this horse's greatness lay in his lovely temperament, in the fact that he did not get unduly 'fussed up', that he was a good doer, that he could race in a relaxed manner. But on the one occasion when he raced twice in just over a week, he was restless and strung up after the second outing, 'weaving' from side to side in his box and making it clear that in his case anyway, 'enough is enough'.

So Brigadier Gerard was raced sufficiently to test him thoroughly, including keeping him in training as a four-year-old, but with sufficient gaps between his engagements to ensure he always came out 'rarin' to go'. His career was undoubtedly aided by the good partnership he formed with Joe Mercer, the jockey who rode him throughout. And his great courage and speed, combined with versatility and the ability to conserve himself until asked for an effort, helped him overcome any lack of inherent stamina in races much longer than the eight to ten furlongs that were probably his ideal distance.

Until the accident that put Mill Reef out of racing, the Mellon colt was always Brigadier Gerard's great rival, and in some ways the over-lapping careers of these two flat-racing giants were reminiscent of those of Arkle and Mill House, the steeplechasing champions.

There was the same rising pressure of excitement from racing and general public alike, a stimulating interest that dominated each season where the two should supposedly meet. There were the two camps of opinion, that of the followers of the majestic, seemingly unconquerable Brigadier Gerard, that of the enthusiastic supporters of the superlative little Mill Reef. The owners, trainers and jockeys of both horses appeared equally confident of the results of any contests. And when, through unforeseen circumstances the only time they did meet was in the Two Thousand Guineas, and the Brigadier won by three lengths, then as on the occasion when Mill House beat Arkle, both the running of the race and its result were interpreted according to which camp you belonged. But there the similarity between the two sets of champions ends, and in this case there was none of the sad eclipse of one by the other as happened when Arkle galloped so quickly into the ascendency.

Although, without any undue planning, but for an accident the paths of Brigadier Gerard and Mill Reef would undoubtedly have crossed again, they were very different types, bred initially for different purposes, and only alike in their pre-eminence over all contemporaries. On balance they must and will both go down in flat-racing history as wonderfully versatile and courageous horses, and the outstanding champions of the decade. Their new contest, success at stud, is only just beginning.

The last date in the racing calendar when public interest was reaching fever pitch over a meeting between these two horses, was the day of the Benson and Hedges Gold Cup at York, in August 1972. In the event, by the date itself Mill Reef was out of racing for ever, and Brigadier Gerard came to the line-up with a record of fifteen wins out of fifteen races behind him and, in the absence of his great rival, apparently invincible in the eyes of the 34,000 people there to watch him in person, and the millions more looking in on television. But horses are not machines, and their occasional unpredictability is what adds spice to the racing scene, and makes every good horseman aware that the partnership into which he enters is one of flesh and blood.

It was not the weather, not like the rain at the previous month's Eclipse that high-lighted Brigadier Gerard's only 'Achilles heel', the heavy ground that destroys the power of his action, so that twice over only his great heart had pulled him through. It could have been that the strain of six races in three months, for all his magnificent appearance in the paddock, was beginning to tell. But principally it was that Roberto, that year's undistinguished Derby winner who had run shockingly in the Irish Sweeps Derby and was to fail twice in France, chose to make that day his own – and ran with a brilliance never to be seen again to shatter the Brigadier's proud record of never being beaten.

Brigadier Gerard's next and last race before bowing out from the racing stage, was at Newmarket towards the end of October that year, when Joe Mercer brought him home to register their final victory, in the Champion Stakes. Now, his racing career behind him, this champion is standing at the Egerton Stud at Newmarket. And if, unlike the delightful story-book character whose name he bears, the 'Adventures' of this particular Brigadier Gerard have been few, if any, his 'exploits' in the sport of kings shine with a brilliance few will ever equal. The years to come will show whether he imbues his offspring with his own splendid qualities.

7
AUREOLE

Whatever the current stallion in residence may be, the buildings and yards of the Royal Stud at Sandringham remain dominated by the statue of a horse long dead, by the huge, weathered, bronze likeness of Persimmon, King Edward VII's almost legendary racehorse. But since 1955 the nearby Wolferton Stud has centred round an animal now well into his twenties but very much alive, the famous Aureole, the pride of the royal Thoroughbreds and the Queen's own acknowledged favourite.

Aureole was bred in 1950 by the Queen's father, the late King George VI. His ancestry includes such renowned names as St Simon and Minoru, Blenheim, Gainsborough and Donatello II. He was the first foal of the royal mare Angelola, and fathered by the immortal little 1933 Derby winner, the then nineteen-year-old Hyperion who was one of the most successful sires of all time.

Aureole, considerably taller than Hyperion, stands 16-1 hands and is a chestnut with a white blaze and three white socks. In old age he has lost none of his 'presence', and surveys domain and people alike with an air distinctly regal. He does make a concession to the years by growing an increasingly thick winter coat against the cold, but in summer is satin smooth, his colour as rich as in the days when he was racing. His legs are clean, and when something excites his interest

Aureole trots off to investigate, head up, full of life, with much of the beauty and elegance of youth. Temperamentally he is no longer quite the spirited handful he used to be but, never a 'boy's horse', continues to demand the experienced attention of a man well versed in the ways of stallions in general, and of this one in particular. His own 'lad', who by 1972 had been doing horses for around fifty years and stallions since he was nineteen, has been with Aureole ever since the horse first arrived at Wolferton.

Some of the mellow Wolferton buildings are older than others and, in winter especially, the atmosphere has a flavour of Victorian tranquillity, an oasis in time, set in the heart of the unspoiled Norfolk countryside and aloof from the noisy hustle of the modern age. These are the conditions under which the Queen, at Sandringham House for the Christmas holiday, most enjoys coming to see Aureole, in the peace that is conspicuous for its absence in her public life.

In these months the forty-three boxes and 150 acres that comprise the stud are as quiet and peaceful as the surrounding countryside, but the picture has changed by 14-15 February, when the breeding season starts. That is when the mares booked to Aureole begin to arrive, coming in by horse-box from different parts of the country, sometimes one or two from overseas. Then Wolferton becomes a hive of industry, with staff working full time, seven days a week and the stud groom on call twenty-four hours a day.

By April when the Queen, if she can find the time, likes to make a short visit to Sandringham there is a crop of lively, new season's foals for her to meet when she drives over to visit Aureole.

When Aureole first arrived at this little Norfolk hamlet the antics he was prone to get up to on the race-course, particularly as a three-year-old, were still fresh in mind. But although he continued his habit of rearing, and will do so today if upset, and is certainly a strong, robust character who needs to be understood, he has no real vice in him. He had no intention of deliberately striking at his lad on the occasion some years ago when he reared up in his box at sight of a mare being led down the road. It was just bad luck that his attendant should have been stooping to pick up a bowl of corn at that moment, and was accidentally knocked down and had his ear torn by the edge of the horse's shoe.

Most animals, two legged or four, have their foibles and Aureole is no exception. He makes no fuss about being shod—he only wears shoes in front—but woe betide anyone trying to stop him going back into the corner on the right hand side of his box, to lean there as he always has, while the blacksmith deals with his off-side. And when it comes to anything a little out of the ordinary, then it's a case of look out for fireworks!

A few years back a regulation during a bad epidemic of Foot and Mouth disease made it obligatory, for people and animals alike, to pass over a disinfecting area, if moving from one part of a farm or estate to another entailed crossing a road. Aureole viewed the thick layer of straw, soaked in disinfectant, that lay between his box and his paddock with the utmost distaste. And since nothing in the world would induce him to set hoof on it, to keep him within the law an entirely new entrance had to be constructed. With such a suspicious and determined character, it was perhaps providential that in his racing days starting stalls were not yet used!

Aureole might have become a truly difficult horse if he had been treated in the old way, now going out of fashion, when a stallion was kept cooped up in its box during the season and all through the winter, its only exercise a daily one-or two-hour stint led out in hand along the public highway. Small wonder that so many of these frustrated animals reacted not unlike the tigers they were reputed to be, and how few might have become really dangerous if, from the start of their stud careers they had been given the kind of freedom that Aureole enjoys.

By night he sleeps in a high, roomy box where his name, the royal cipher, and a giant horseshoe for luck adorn one wall. Early each morning, unless first required for breeding duties, he is led through the yard and across the road to the two-acre paddock with the comfortable shelter that he has always inhabited. The now disused railway runs beyond the further side of the field, and in the old days when the season was commencing and some mares came by train, Aureole always knew from the first moment a train hove in sight way down the track, whether it was carrying members of his new harem. If he decided it was he moved at once to a strategic position overlooking the little station, from which he could cast a critical eye over prospective wives as they were detrained. Nowadays he is equally quick to spot the horse-boxes, and watches with interest as each mare is unloaded to come into the yard.

He has the liberty to roll at will and to wander in and out of shelter as he wishes. Minimal grooming preserves the waterproofing grease in his coat, and the fact that he is out in all weathers—he has never been known to shiver on even the coldest, snowiest day—has kept him physically hard and tough, while the advantage of being able to watch and take an interest in all that goes on, keeps him mentally occupied and happy. Exercise is voluntary, taken when he feels so inclined. Often in the afternoon when it is time for the mares to be led down the road from the paddocks to their boxes in the yard, Aureole sets off on his self-imposed routine for keeping fit, trotting round and round the wide circles to be seen in his paddock, that are sometimes pounded so deep that they have to be filled in.

For years Aureole's destructive taste for wood was a problem. He was quite capable of gnawing through, in a few hours, one of the palings that fence him in, and some of the rails still bear proof of the habit. An ingenious idea, of thin wires carrying a low, two-volt electrical charge that run along the edges of the wooden rails, put paid to it. But Aureole lost no time in gauging to a nicety how to turn his lean, aristocratic head sideways so as to avoid them, as he pokes it through the fence to receive the offerings of sugar nobs and carrots he has always considered his due. He has in fact always been encouraged to do this, because it was found in the early days that he reared and played up if caught in the conventional manner, but has never taken exception to having a rein attached to his head-collar from the outside of the fence. The flow of titbits can then continue, while his lad and an assistant climb through the rails and bridle him. Possibly with age he would now consent to being caught in a more usual manner, but there seems little point in abandoning a tried method that works well.

In his stud duties Aureole is intelligent and easy to handle, and very quiet with his mares. His virile parent Hyperion fathered two foals at the age of twenty-nine, and although this is exceptional, Aureole, for the 1973 season when he was twenty-three, had thirty-five mares booked to him at a fee of 1,000 guineas each.

Many stallions tend to sire better foals of one sex than the other. The 1954 Derby winner, Never Say Die, fathers good fillies but unexceptional colts, and while no-one was interested in the colts of that good horse Abernant, his fillies were first class. Aureole follows much the same trend, but in reverse. He has had two good fillies, Aurabella, winner of the Irish Oaks, and Paysanne who dead-heated with the subsequent Prix de l'Arc de Triomphe winner, San San, to win the 1972 Prix Vermeille, but it is for his colts that he is famed.

Saint Crispin III, his first foal, now in Japan, was a winner of the Prix de l'Arc de Triomphe and of the Eclipse Stakes, before becoming a notable sire in his own right. Other sons include the famous St Paddy, now another leading sire, who won the Derby, St Ledger and Eclipse Stakes; Aurelius and Provoke who both in turn won the St Ledger; the Queen's good horse Hopeful Venture, a winner in France and in the Hardwicke Stakes, and Vienna who sired the celebrated Vaguely Noble. Aureole was Leading Sire in 1960 and 1961, and second in 1965. In 1971 his yearlings averaged 8,000 guineas each, and 6,750 guineas a year later. But before he came to Wolferton to earn fame through his progeny, this worthy son of Hyperion carried the royal colours to victory in seven races, and won a total £42,000 in prize money, including place money.

On the race-course Aureole was a handful. He boiled up with the excitement of the crowds, and the royal jockey, Harry Carr, came to know only too well the spectacular rearings and plungings, sometimes accompanied with an overt threat not to start at all, that usually preceded a race. But horses often run differently for different jockeys, and although Aureole was never to be the easiest of rides, he responded to Eph Smith's methods more kindly than to those of Harry Carr.

Smith was first asked to ride for the Queen when the royal jockey could not do the weight for Aureole in the 1953 Cumberland Lodge Stakes at Ascot. He had just won the St Ledger, a race in which Aureole was third, and three years previously had won the Yorkshire Oaks for King George VI with the royal filly, Above Board. But although fully appreciative of the honour, Smith was very aware of how difficult the Queen's horse could be if he chose, and he felt it would be wise to make sure he could get on with the chestnut and do him justice, before once more accepting a ride in the royal colours.

The Queen's trainer, at the time Captain Boyd Rochford, therefore agreed that Smith should ride Aureole at work before making up his mind, and the jockey was able to try out an idea for coming to terms with the horse.

A successful jockey is not necessarily a good horseman, but Eph Smith was one who combined the two, and he had seen enough of Aureole's racing as a two-year-old to feel sure that, although the horse pulled very hard, it had an exceptionally light mouth. Constant pulling and jerking by both mount and jockey must cause such a horse considerable pain and could well be the root cause of some of the troubles, but the problem was how to retain control without too much hand movement.

When Smith took Aureole on their trial run on Newmarket Heath, therefore, the horse, at his request was wearing a neckstrap, and by twining his fingers in it the jockey was able to refrain from tearing at the horse's mouth. Certainly Aureole went much more kindly, and when, on the strength of this Smith agreed to take the ride at Ascot, the neckstrap was in place and no doubt proved an aid to a good win by a length and a half.

Eph Smith was retained as Aureole's jockey for the wonderful season's racing the chestnut then achieved as a four-year-old. It began with a rather unlucky second place at Sandown but he then took the Coronation Cup at Epsom with great ease, and followed that up by winning the Hardwicke Stakes at Ascot. The biggest triumph was winning the £27,500 prize for first place in the King George VI and Queen Elizabeth Stakes.

There was no doubt the horse and Eph Smith achieved a mutually beneficial partnership, but even so it was not accomplished without a few traumas. The horse was not one to take kindly to the whip, and Smith was instructed by Captain Boyd Rochford that Aureole was not to be touched. At work one day, however, the chestnut started getting up to his old tricks, rearing and refusing to go on, and the jockey, taking a chance that the 'Captain' was otherwise engaged, landed his horse one behind the girth, at the same time letting out an intimidating roar to 'Get on with you!'

The unexpected treatment worked well on that occasion, and was employed once more at the start of a race soon after when Aureole obviously began to contemplate going up instead of going forward. But his jockey had only to show him the whip and growl menacingly for his mount to recollect, change his ideas, and quickly comply.

The only other time Smith used his whip on Aureole was in the final stages of the Hardwicke Sakes, when Manny Mercer, coming up fast and close on a French horse, started to gain a slight lead. Aureole always hated being challenged by a horse right alongside and instead of quickening, laid back his ears and seemed about to drop the bit and fall behind. With a horse of his temperament using the whip at such a moment could have strengthened Aureole in his resolve, but instead he responded and raced on again to win while Mercer, himself hampered by his tactics of riding so close, was unable to draw his own whip at all.

Undoubtedly good hands were the main key to Eph Smith's success with Aureole, and the horse was appreciative of being ridden as though the bit in his mouth was made of silk, but there was a moment before the start of the King George VI and Queen Elizabeth Stakes when hands were of small avail, and it seemed as though the Queen's horse might not even be in the line-up. When he started to play up in front of the stands Smith had taken him out of the parade, and was making direct for the starting gate when Aureole took exception to the sudden raising of an umbrella, and deposited his jockey unceremoniously on the ground. The immediate reaction of the majority of high-mettled thoroughbreds on finding themselves free, would be to high-tail it for the horizon, but Aureole, always a law unto himself, chose instead to stop and graze, as unperturbed as a pet pony whose child rider has just rolled off its back. And when Smith approached him, optimistically holding out another offering of Ascot grass, this horse that normally rears and creates a turmoil if not caught from outside the paddock fence, allowed his jockey to grab the reins and jump back into the saddle.

The only real disappointment of Aureole's racing career was that he was second in the 1953 Derby instead of winning it. Apart from its value in stake money and the enormous prestige of the winner being proved the undisputed best three-year-old in the world, there is a flavour attached to the Blue Riband of the turf that makes Derby Day an occasion distinct from all other racing dates. Whether or not they are part of the colourful crowd that has been swelling in size to mill about on the Epsom Downs since the small hours; whether they are one of the élite, eligible to stroll decorously on the holy turf of the paddock; whether they have arrived by Rolls Royce or by special train; whether their coach was of the motorised variety, or one of those few splendid relics of the past, a coach-and-four, that still turn out for such a day; whether they are sitting in the stands, or on the grass of the Downs, on top of one of the topless buses that provide a first-class view, or whether they are at home sitting glued to the 'telly', the British people treat Derby Day as a national event. And in 1953 Derby Day possessed a more potent magic than usual, because it was Coronation Year and the Queen's horse was running. A royal win would have been immensely popular, but Aureole went down to the giant Pinza, Sir Gordon Richard's first, and only, Derby winner.

Yet if Pinza was the victor on the race-course, Aureole has had his revenge a hundred-fold since. Where Pinza proved of little worth at stud, Aureole has triumphed. His successful progeny are all over the world, and based on the statistical records for 1972, it is estimated that Aureole has sired the winners of 500 world-wide races, with a total value of one million pounds.

Although the Queen is justly proud of her handsome chestnut horse, and proud too of the great record of his progeny, her interest is not confined to monetary values. As always it is the horse himself that chiefly concerns her. She has a great affection for Aureole, and would not dream of being at Sandringham without going to see him, and by the looks of her favourite horse this is something she should be able to do for some years yet. Aureole is old, but he is in fine fettle, and although there was some idea of semi-retiring him to Sandringham and bringing Ribero to Wolferton in his stead, the plan was dropped. On second thoughts it was felt that the chestnut might well fret at leaving the only home he has known since his retirement from racing, and now Aureole is assured of spending his remaining years in the surroundings where he knows he belongs.

8
GOLDEN MILLER

When Red Rum won the 1973 Grand National in 9 minutes 1·9 seconds he broke, by almost 19 seconds, the race record that had stood for nearly thirty-nine years. For it was in 1934 that Golden Miller, making his second attempt, gained a victory at Aintree in the best time performance to date and when carrying the burden of 12 st 2 lb.

The Miller's win was the greater triumph for having failed to complete the course in the previous year and because, except for that '34 win and the second place he took in the Becher's Chase two years later when ridden by Fulke Walwyn, he never again got round Aintree. But then he was a horse of sense and sensibility, he did not like the course or, at any rate some of the fences, and being one who knew his own mind made his antipathy very plain. His achievements in other races on other courses alone turned Golden Miller, in his time, into the racing legend he remains.

On the face of it the strong bay horse with the grand proportions, the white star on his forehead, the big, close-tipped ears and super-intelligent eye, did not come of very spectacular stock, although a delve far back into his parent's ancestry shows that both could claim kinship with at least one distinguished line. But his dam, Miller's Pride, although she bred some useful horses in addition to his illustrious self, never won a race. And although his sire, Gold Court, also fathered the winner of the Irish Grand National, neither he nor his father before him ever graced a race-course. The stud fee to Gold Court that produced his famous son was just £5.

There were no fanfares to herald the Miller's birth in Ireland in 1927. He was foaled in an old shed, spent his first year running out with cattle in a big field, and as a yearling was sold at the Ballsbridge Sales, to the breeder of his sire, for not much more than 100 guineas. He changed hands again as three-year-old, and was then backed and given a little elementary education. Not long afterwards he arrived in England at the Longstowe training stables run by a young man called Bristowe, who had bought the horse unseen on the strength of its being half-brother to an excellent animal he had owned, and lately sold.

To put it mildly, Bristowe was not favourably impressed by the first sight of his new purchase. The journey from Ireland had been a long and exhausting one, and the awkward-looking youngster, hairy and much in need of grooming, that was eyeing him with a mixture of depression and apprehension from the depths of the box, seemed to bear small resemblance to the smart young potential 'chaser he was expecting.

By the end of the following winter Golden Miller had done little to alter his trainer's original notions. He had shown no turn of foot on the gallops, and his apparent lethargy or lack of speed was borne out in his one and only race, on the flat, in that autumn. Next he was taken hunting, and if it was too much to expect such a green, gangling youngster to jump and gallop like a seasoned hunter, at least it was felt the experience would interest and sharpen him up. But the Miller had inherited his mother's placid nature, and all his life was to take things much as they came. And where this trait was to prove a blessing amongst the hurly-burly of the racecourse, or on the streets of cities through which he had to be walked after arriving by train for a meeting, it was exasperating that neither the thrilling sound of the horn nor the music of hounds, nor the squelch and drumming of many other hooves made any impact on this horse at all. He made no effort to keep up with the hounds, and had little success in going over the jumps rather than through them. Frankly he liked hunting as little as he was one day to like that course at Aintree, but for all the jumping blunders of the day, the Miller was already showing an aptitude for keeping on his feet – a trait for which he would become renowned.

When Golden Miller and his feature and final owner, the Hon. Dorothy Paget, eventually caught up with each other, it is hard to say which became the most famous. Probably both were destined for fame in any case, although in most ways the horse's has outlived his owner's, but the colour this wealthy, eccentric woman and her splendid horse brought to the racing scene was irresistable, and altogether they were to hold the stage from the season of 1931-2 until the February of 1939. But before that partnership came into being there were to be six races for Golden Miller in the ownership of a Mr Carr; the switching of Dorothy Paget's sporting interests from racing mechanised horse-power to that involving flesh and blood; and a big change of heart for the Miller's trainer, Briscoe.

The first races were over hurdles and resulted in a promising third place in heavy going, followed by two wins, one on good going, one when it was soft. The Miller then tried his hand at steeplechasing, and quickly proved that he could jump the big fences with the same effortless ease he showed in brushing through the flights of hurdles. One bad mistake landed his jockey up on his neck, but he made little of it and was only just beaten into second place. He might in fact have won if he had been ridden out forcefully by someone with less knowledge of the hurt to his spirit that whip and heels could do, at that stage of his career, to such a promising young horse. By now the Miller was condescending to show what he could really do in the way of speed on the home gallops, and that was a pity because it tempted his trainer to try him in a couple of two mile races on the flat. This was not the horse's scene, and he came in an inglorious eighth in the first, and was fourth out of eight runners in the other.

Up to that date, between 1 September 1930 and 16 April 1931, the Miller had participated in seven races, and galloped and jumped his way round thirteen and a half miles. It seemed he had earned a rest and he was put out to grass. Meanwhile, at the request of Mr Carr, by then tragically ill, Golden Miller was sold. The horse had come on the market at a moment when his trainer's opinion of him had swung from zero to a very high mark indeed, and around the time when the second daughter of Lord Queensborough had decided to exchange the thrills of owning a fleet of racing cars for those of possessing a stud of racehorses. It was coincidence that led Dorothy Paget to Briscoe and so to Golden Miller, and it was unprecedented luck for the trainer that when he offered her what he described as 'the best steeplechase horse in the world', his boast should turn out to be the unvarnished truth.

The Miller first carried his new owner's colours, the quickly famous blue with a yellow hoop on body and sleeves and yellow cap with a blue hoop, at Cheltenham, in an unpretentious hurdle race which he won. He was third in another, and won the next before forsaking hurdling forever for his proper sphere of steeplechasing.

The race chosen for his second debut was a tough one for all its title of the Moderate Steeplechase. And the fact that, owing to a muddle by Briscoe over the weights the Miller was disqualified, did nothing to diminish the way in which he won, slamming an opposition that included Forbra, the winner of that season's Grand National. The mix-up had also left Golden Miller still with novice status, and before he lost it he had won another novice 'chase and come second in the other.

By now the Miller was a magnificent horse, an acknowledged up and coming young 'chaser, with enormous strength and stamina and an economical method of fencing, fast and low and off his fore-hand that spelt success. He was not yet at the zenith of his many wonderful seasons, but he was rapidly slipping into first gear. Yet for all his growing reputation Golden Miller was thought to have little chance in that Cheltenham Gold Cup of '32. And even when he won, the pundits considered that luck had been with him, and the falling of the favourite and another well-rated horse had been the chief contribution to his victory.

Golden Miller set out to prove them wrong – very wrong: he won that race in 1932, '33, '34, '35 and '36, five Gold Cups in a row, and with those triumphs filled in the time between with fourteen wins in nineteen other races. Though some doubted it, he was only flesh and blood, and so there were three 'places' in three additional races to be counted in, a second, and two thirds – one of those in a flat race –

and he ran out, in the Newbury Chase, a fortnight before Cheltenham in '36.

Then in 1934 there was the greatest triumph of all, winning the
Grand National in the same year as the Cheltenham Gold Cup, a feat
never achieved before and the crown of a horse's versatility. He was
only seven years old, which is young for Aintree, and he won by five
lengths, eight seconds faster than Kellosboro' Jack who had beaten
the time record the previous year, and carrying 7lb. more. It was a
wonderful victory by a magnificent horse that by then had become
something of a national institution. It seems sad that eventually
Golden Miller could not be allowed to rest on that one laurel, particularly when he had so many other victor's garlands to collect in
other fields.

Of course the function of a racehorse is to race, and with high
hopes and apparently unarguable grounds for thinking he might win
the National two years running – he had won all of his five previous
races – there was good reason for entering him again in 1935. But
after that?

In 1933 he had made such a bad mistake at Beecher's that he lost
his confidence, blundered even more badly at the following fence and
unshipped his jockey. All horses have good, sometimes too good mem-
ories, and for all his brilliant win next time, the Miller would not
have forgotten. And although that year he was extra fit and everything went well, there were many to think even so that the horse's
style of jumping, that low, economical leap off his forehand, was not
really suited to the huge fences and steep 'pitch' at Aintree. Maybe he
knew it too.

He came to the Grand National in 1935 after again winning the
Gold Cup, but this time the Cheltenham race had been a tough, hard
one, a desperate dual to the finish with Thomond II and victory only
wrested by three-quarters of a length. It must have taken a lot out of
him and the line up for the National came fifteen days later.

There are several different versions of exactly what happened that
day. It has been said he was never going 'right' from the moment the
tapes went up; or that he always took time to warm up but was then
going as well as usual. As he came to the fateful open ditch after
Valentine's some say there was an obvious thought of refusing, some

put it as a hesitation in his stride, or that there was a duck to the left, a screwing in his take-off, the jump even more left-handed as he landed, or that the leap he made after partially dislodging his jockey was so enormous that the result was inevitable. Whatever it was no rider could have sat him, and the end product was the same and Golden Miller and his jockey parted company.

When the runners came into sight again from the far side of the course and it was realised the Miller was not there, the crowds were stunned. Within minutes of the finish of the race there were recriminations between owner and trainer, the jockey reiterated his conviction that the Miller had not been 'right' before the race, vets were summoned. They found nothing wrong, and the very next day the horse went down to the start for another race at Aintree, the Championship 'Chase.

But Golden Miller had had enough. He went no further than the first fence, one of the smaller National obstacles, and there his half-hearted attempt at a jump again unshipped his jockey.

This time the row and unpleasantness were much worse. It culminated in Golden Miller's sudden removal, at Briscoe's own request, from the trainer who had had him in his proud, anxious care ever since the horse first came to England, in a parting from the lovely dog, a Great Dane, that had become his boon companion, and of going eventually to the stables of a new trainer, Owen Anthony.

The Miller was turned out and given a rest, then brought back gently to his mission in life. At the end of December 1935 he won the unpretentious Andover Handicap at Newbury, in a manner that made Meyrick Good of the Sporting Life acclaim him 'better than ever' – an opinion he was to rescind a couple of months later when the Miller, going easily and for no apparent reason, ran out at the fifth fence from home in the Newbury Chase.

They said he had become cunning, they said he had a kink, so Golden Miller went to Cheltenham, the course that he loved, and pricked his big ears and took his fifth, and last, Gold Cup by twelve lengths.

Fifteen days later they brought him again to Aintree for the National. At the first fence an outsider jumped and fell just ahead of him and brought him down – for the only time in his whole career. He was remounted and set off after the field, jumping impeccably until after Valentine's second time round where he met his bogey fence again, began to jink and stopped. A week later he ran really well at Cardiff to take third place in the Welsh Grand National.

In November of the 1936-7 season Fulke Walwyn rode Golden Miller at Liverpool in the Becher Chase. He admired his mount as a marvellous old horse, but he did not find him an easy ride. By then the Miller was a very 'sticky' jumper at Aintree, but Fulke got him round, for only the second time in all the horse's attempts at Liverpool, and they took second place. In the following spring the Miller was there again – for the National.

Since his last attempt he had won four of his interim six races and been placed in the other two, so he had not been wasting his time. They should have known their horse better than to make him have another go, and this time he finally convinced them. From the moment he came over Valentine's he made it crystal clear to jockey and onlookers alike that he had no intention of attempting the fence he really hated.

In his next season, up to 10 March, Golden Miller ran five times. He was unplaced once, second twice, and won the rest. Out of these the Prince's Chase, a valuable one, was taken in atrocious weather. The Miller loved the mud but this was deep going, and he battled to the finish, refusing to give in. It was a great race but it seemed to take too much out of him, and without showing any of his old fire he was well beaten in his next. Finished? they asked. Not yet, said Golden Miller, and took the Optional Selling 'Chase at Birmingham by twenty-five lengths.

At last there was to be no more Aintree, but the old fellow would like to have another go at Cheltenham. To those in the know the Miller was not the horse he used to be. How could he be? He was by then eleven years old and this was at the end of his eighth racing season. But the crowds waived all that and came in their thousands to do the champion honour. And the Miller so nearly made it. It was only in the last straight that youth triumphed over age, and there was nothing sad in his defeat to second place.

Cheltenham was the Miller's swan song. He made that clear in his one other race in the February of '39, and so that one can be discounted and his career finished on the course that he had made his own. He lived happily in retirement with his close friend, Insurance, another of Miss Paget's horses. They made dual and obviously enjoyed appearances at such apposite entertainments as the International Horse Show, and he ended his life at the age of thirty when he had to be put down.

Golden Miller won twenty-eight of his fifty-three races, was placed in a dozen more, and when be bungled it was usually because of the unwisdom of humans in running him where he had no wish to run. He is a legend and deserves to be, and the highest tribute that can be paid to any steeplechaser is the supposition, so far never proved: 'Could this one be another Golden Miller'?

9
FREEBOOTER

By 1839 the big race at Aintree, first run three years previously for 'gentlemen only' and with a field of four, had become the steeple-chasing event of the year. Crowds converged to watch; there was an entry of fifty-five with seventeen horses going to the start, amongst them the soon-to-be-famous Lottery, the favourite; a mare called The Nun, considered a bit plump and therefore galloped extensively just before the race – and Conrad, the mount of a certain Captain Becher who had won in 1836. The going varied from growing crops to heavy plough, the obstacles from light fencing to a formidable wall, con-structed of stone topped with turf and standing five foot high, which provided the onlookers in the nearby stands with their fill of excite-ment. There were plenty of thrills and spills on other parts of the course and numerous refusals, and when Conrad, with no mind for a six-foot-wide brook with palings and a high hedge in front, tumbled headlong in, the redoubtable Captain Becher took a toss as spec-tacular as it was wetting, and all unknowingly gave his name to the fence and to posterity. One horse was killed during the race, and Lot-tery won it with prophetic ease.

By the next year the title of the contest, the 'Grand Liverpool Stee-plechase', had become the 'Grand National', a shortened version invented by a reporter writing up the 1839 results. This time there was a horrible series of mishaps at the notorious wall, but an Irish horse called Valentine was one of the few that managed to remain on its feet. Its rider had boasted he would be first at the obstacle and the pace he set was the chief cause of the disasters there, but although, perhaps with justice, Valentine did not win it did finish, and like Captain Becher its name, as Valentine's Brook, has been immortalised in one of the National's most famous jumps.

Through the next decade the fortunes of the Grand National went up and down. At times the toll of horses sparked off adverse public reaction, at times the blatant bribery and corruption brought all steeplechasing, and the National in particular, into disrepute. Yet by 1843, despite the sport still being considered by many a discreditable and unsavoury poor relation of flat-racing, the course at Aintree was designed in a form that would be little changed for a century, the stands were finished, and the site was declared one of the best in the country.

Towards the end of the nineteenth century steeplechasing got a welcome boost from the interest of the Prince of Wales, soon to be King Edward VII. In 1896 he had won the Derby with Persimmon, and when his 'chaser Ambush won the Grand National four years later, the Prince received the tremendous acclamation of a fervently royalist crowd, and the race gained the royal accolade. From then on, although often to be the centre of further, sometimes acrimonious controversy, the National became in the rapidly developing world of steeple-chasing what the Derby is to flat-racing, and remained so, off and on, until the slight decline in prestige, with owners if not with the public, of recent years.

The names of the famous, the horses that have won the National, ring down the years with a clarion as clear as those of the Derby winners – even though with few exceptions (the winner in 1855 was a stallion, and so was the 1909 winner, Lutteur III) entires are not normally raced over fences, and therefore a steeplechaser's renown cannot usually be perpetuated in his progeny.

Usually the race has proved too tough for the minority of gallant mares that take part, and between 1841 when Charity beat the field, and 1951 when the small Nickel Coin benefited from the general fiasco to win from the only other horse left standing, only ten 'ladies'

Above No horse was ever more aware of his own indisputable claim to be a champion than the great Arkle

Right A great steeplechaser and splendid jumper, Mill House was fated to race during the era of the indomitable Arkle

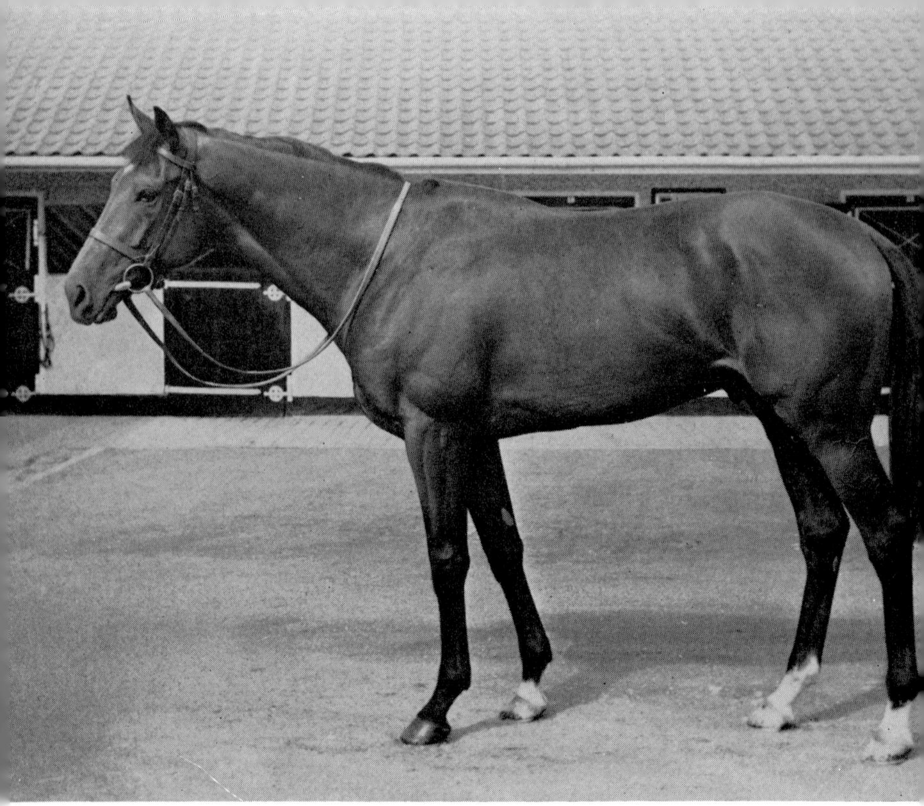

Above The Canadian-bred Nijinsky is one of the few elite to have won the Triple Crown – The Two Thousand Guineas, the Derby and the St Leger

Left Mandarin, with Fred Winter up, in the Grand Steeplechase de Paris 1962 which he won despite the handicap of a broken bit

Opposite, above Mill Reef, an American colt, turned out to be one of the greatest mile-and-a-half horses of all time. His racing career ended with a broken foreleg

Right The Queen's horse, Aureole (nearest the rails), winning the King George VI and Queen Elizabeth Stakes in 1954

17

Golden Miller winning the Grand National in 1934 by five lengths, in the same year that he also won the Cheltenham Gold Cup

A horse who made a speciality of Aintree was Freebooter, who won the National, the Champion and Becher 'chases, and the Sefton twice, in the days before the fences were modified

Phar Lap, the New Zealand horse who dominated the Australian racing scene from 1929 to 1932 and who died in mysterious circumstances in the USA

Above The Arab stallion, Indian Magic, one of the most famous products of the Crabbet Stud owned by Lady Wentworth

Left The great show-jumper, Foxhunter, who did so much to popularize the sport and was the first horse of his trade to become a household name

Left Doublet and Princess Anne at Burghley in 1971 on their way to becoming European Individual Champions

Below Lochinvar at the Burghley Three Day Event in 1964; he was one of Major Allhusen's famous trio of Event horses and won a silver medal in the Mexico Olympics

Opposite, above A brilliant, if erratic, jumper, Lucky Strike could clear seven foot with ease

Below, right Marian Coates on Stroller, the pony whose superlative spring enabled him to challenge the most famous show-jumpers of his era

Above, left Psalm and his rider Anne Moore—a successful partnership that represented Britain in the 1972 Olympics where they won a silver medal
Above, right Pretty Polly, a champion herself, is also the founder of a line of champion ponies

Below The American pacer, Albatross, who by his retirement in 1972 had won more prize money in a single season than any other harness horse and was the fastest racing Standardbred in the American history of the sport have won the National.

There have been National winners of all kinds and makes and shapes and ages. In the very beginning steeplechasing, as such, was the favoured pursuit of dare-devil 'bloods' matching their hunters against each other across country, over any route they considered the shortest between the chosen churches. In 1837 the winner of the National was described as a 'hunting cob'; that of 1852 as a 'rat of a thing'. But if the very speed of the developing sport soon put paid to anything quite as unlikely as that, there have still been plenty of surprising winners. Troytown, hero of 1920 was a distinguished 'chaser of his time but gained the dubious title of the most difficult of all National rides; the huge Master Robert, the winner in 1924, was considered so hopelessly slow that he spent part of his previous career as a plough horse; a bargain yearling that cost £50 grew up to be the famous Tipperary Tim that won at 100–1 in 1928; and Forbra, a flat-race reject, was the winner in 1932. Six years later an American 'pony' stallion called Battleship, ridden by a seventeen-year-old, came in first by one stride.

The altered entry conditions of 1932 – which laid down that to qualify, a horse must have been placed in a steeplechase not less than three miles in length and worth a minimum of £200 to the winner – cut out the really impossible participants, but of all races, luck plays a big part in the National and this is one of its fascinating aspects. Way back in 1911 it was a series of disasters to other runners that made the one-eyed outsider Glenside a winner; in 1921 Shaun Spadah was the only horse to remain on his feet throughout, and at least one incredible National result is still fresh in memory. That was in 1967 when the riderless Popham Down, at Fence Twenty-three caused the collapse of all bar one of the remaining runners, and the totally unconsidered Foinavon was left to win by fifteen lengths, to his own and his jockey's amazement and the jubilation of those punters who were given odds of 445–1 on the Tote.

So much for the oddities, so much for the chances in the world's most famous steeplechase. Those with knowledge who wish to buy or back a horse likely to win the National will look for a compact animal with good bone, and the lean head that denotes breeding. For if the breeding of a 'chaser is not quite the same as for a flat-racer, some go back, on either the sire's or the dam's side to aristocrats that have been involved with the Derby, and for years the majority of good jumpers have acquired their speed and stamina from an intake of blue blood. Those who wish to study what might be called the true National type, could do no better than to track down a photograph of a horse called Freebooter.

He was foaled in County Wexford, Ireland, in 1941, and was by Steelpoint – leading sire in 1950, famous for his jumping progeny – out of a mare called Proud Fury. And since Freebooter's great-grand-dam, Imamzarine, was by the Arabian Imanzade, he was one of the few racehorses to have had a re-introduction of Arabian blood.

A well-knit horse with great loins and quarters and beautifully sloped shoulders, Freebooter was deep through and thickset, standing on short, clean legs that made him appear smaller than he was. Bought by Mrs Brotherton who lives in Yorkshire, and trained by the Yorkshire specialist in 'chasers, Bobby Renton, Freebooter came to the fore as a maiden by winning the since discontinued Victory Chase at Manchester. And it was chiefly due to this horse's successes that Mrs Brotherton headed the list of winning owners for the National Hunt Racing season of 1949–50.

In character he was a charming, friendly animal, as attached to the humans in his life as to the cat companion that lived in his stable. He also had his share of brains, and when a hock injury, the result of a bad fall when standing off too far at the Canal Turn in the 1952 National, made him lame for a long time, he solved the difficulty he then had of getting up from his rest, by using intelligence: the horse's lad and all the stable staff became used to listening for Freebooter's distinctive whinny, which said very clearly and a shade imperiously: 'Please would someone come and give me a hand up on to my feet!' Like Arkle he was always keenly aware when it was a racing day, but in his case took his cue from the best suit donned by his stable lad, all spruced up to take the horse to a meeting.

Different types of courses and fences usually suit different types of horse, and even the best of 'chasers normally have their own, acquired or ingrained preferences and dislikes. This is particularly true where Aintree is concerned, and some of the most brilliant jumpers – Golden Miller is the classic example – have taken a rooted objection either to the entire National set-up, or to some special fence or fences. Equally there is the Aintree specialist who obviously finds real joy in tackling such a course, and amongst these Freebooter stands supreme.

In Freebooter's time the Aintree fences were much stiffer than they are now, and none of them had been sloped off or modified as was done in recent years to try and cut down the casualties. It takes a brave horse to tacle the National today, but then it required even more courage and ability. Freebooter learned his way round Aintree, apart from the National, by winning other principal Liverpool Steeplechases – the Champion, the Becher and the Sefton – twice. On the second occasion Freebooter was being saddled for the latter race, the jockey, on that day George Slack, remarked to Bobby Renton that although he had ridden round Aintree many times he had never yet managed a winner. The horse's trainer assured him that his luck should be in this time, and when Freebooter and Slack came into the winners' enclosure, the jockey was able to comment happily that he had just had a conducted tour round the course.

Freebooter's greatest day came on 25 March 1950, when as a nine-year-old he lined up for the Grand National. He had been beaten by a neck at Sandown that January, and a month later, carrying the top weight, had won the Great Yorkshire Handicap at Doncaster. In the National, carrying 11st 11lb and ridden by his usual jockey, J. Power, he started joint favourite, out of forty-nine runners, with Roimond who had finished second in 1949. In the field was the popular Monaveen, the entire that the Queen, then Princess Elizabeth, shared with her mother and who was running in the Princess's colours; so was Cromwell, a good 'chaser ridden by his owner, the popular amateur rider the late Lord Mildmay. Cloncarrig was well fancied and Shagreen had his share of last-minute supporters.

It was one of the years when the first fence took its toll, and seven horses fell. That set the trend, and after the first time round there were only a few left to battle it out.

Freebooter, always a great-hearted horse, was jumping superbly. Over Becher's first time round he landed in front of Monaveen, who finished fifth, Roimond, who was to fall at the next fence, and Acthon Major who was to be third. After Valentine's, Cloncarrig, going well, was leading and for a moment it looked as though there might be an exciting close finish. But he turned turtle at the second to last fence, leaving Freebooter to come safely over the ultimate fence, and then there was only that long, exhausting run-in that has defeated many a potential winner. But Freebooter galloped on, ears pricked, to finish fifteen lengths in front of Wot No Sun, to beat the 1949 winner's time by a fifth of a second, and to add £9,239 to his already considerable share of prize money.

That 4 mile, 856 yard race, with its 30 redoubtable fences – that include the tricky guard-rail and ditch at Number Three, the nerve-testing Becher's, the difficult, dangerous Canal Turn and Valentine's Brook, and the huge Chair where the field funnel in on one another – has no real equal in the world. And the National often takes so much out of a horse that he never wins a good race again, but Freebooter was one of the few exceptions.

As for the National itself, there are gluttons who come back year after year – sometimes without much sensibility on their owner's part – but out of the 110 times the race had been been run between its inception and Freebooter's year, only six horses had won it twice. Freebooter, as an Aintree 'specialist' that genuinely liked the National course, might have made the seventh, but 1951 was one of those years that is remembered as a shambles. The start was a disgrace, and Mrs Brotherton's bay was one of the many that was facing the wrong way and had to be turned to set off well in the rear. The trouble and confusion continued from the first fence on, until only Nickel Coin, the eventual winner, and Royal Tan were left standing.

Freebooter had been brought down through no fault of his own, and continued his successful steeplechasing career through the next season until the National of 1952. His prestige was such that he started favourite, and he was going superbly when, as his jockey said afterwards, over-anxiety caused him to take-off too soon at the calamitous Canal Turn, and he paid the penalty.

After his racing days were over Freebooter retired to Kirkham Abbey, his owner's Yorkshire home, where for a few seasons he became a notable hunter. The old horse really loved the sport and took to it like a duck to water, and his tremendous jumping and tractable nature gave his riders equal enjoyment.

Freebooter lived until he was twenty-four, and in the annals of a course that he made very much his own, his name will never be forgotten.

10
PHAR LAP

Visitors stepping for the first time inside the doors of Australia's Melbourne Museum are sometimes startled at sight of a big chestnut horse, apparently just pausing on its way before moving out past them on to the track. But their justifiable surprise is really an involuntary tribute to the skill of an eminent American taxidermist – and, in turn, his life-like 'sculpture' is a tribute to Phar Lap, still the most famous of all Australia's doughty race-horses.

Created with Phar Lap's hide, the 'statue' was placed in the Museum in 1938, six years after the great horse's mysterious death. And if interest prompts the visitor to probe further, Phar Lap's heart, found after his demise to be eight pounds heavier than that of an ordinary Army remount, is installed in the Institute of Anatomy in Canberra. His skeleton, prepared and obtained with funds raised by horse-loving admirers, is exhibited in the Dominion Museum in Wellington, for Phar Lap was born in New Zealand.

Like Ireland, New Zealand is a country especially suited by soil and climate to the breeding of top-class thoroughbreds. And both factors have contributed through the years, well boosted by such successes as that of the famous sire, Battle Wagon, to the growing inroad now being made into the Japanese and American race-horse market, in addition to the flourishing and now many-year-old export trade to

Australia.

For some time, and particularly since the late 1960s, there has also been a boom in thoroughbred horse breeding in Australia. In the warmer areas of the temperate zone the rainfall and terrain were found to be excellently suited to the purpose, and modern veterinary expertise on the specialised breeding problems of blood mares, combined with research into general equine health and disease, are playing an invaluable part in its increasing success. By 1971 there were around 5,500 individual breeders in Australasia, contributing their vital part to the racing scene that is both a gainful industry and a national sport.

But though the first all-Australian stud book was compiled in 1878, even in the 1920s when Phar Lap was foaled, it was a very different picture from that of today, and for years to come New Zealand-bred horses were to dominate the coveted Classic and Long Distance Australian races. In 1927 it would have been the natural thing for a then little known Sydney trainer called Harry Telford to go to New Zealand, to the Yearling Sales at Trentham, to make a purchase.

He had picked out the animal he wished to buy from its particulars in the Sales Catalogue, his interest fostered by a hunch over its breeding. The colt in question was by Night Raid out of Entreaty, which was not over-exciting, but Telford knew that this meant the blood of Musket, sire of the brilliant horse Carbine, was included on both sides of the pedigree – and he was prepared to gamble on that.

The yearling was eventually knocked down for a price moderate even for those times, but despite this Harry Telford was unable to raise the wind himself and had organised a backer, one David Davis also of Sydney, who duly put up the required £168.

It must have strained Telford's faith in his reading of the animal's blood-lines when he actually saw his proposed purchase in the flesh. For the yearling was an awkward, ugly creature, so unprepossessing that when it eventually arrived by sea from New Zealand, Davis, its disgusted new owner, refused to waste money on having it trained, and Telford had to agree to lease the horse for the next three years. He called it Phar Lap, from the Siamese meaning 'to emit light from the sky', a name that could have been evoked either from an obstinate refusal to admit an apparent mistake, or from an unshakable belief in his own judgement. Either way there seemed precious little light to be conjured from this particular portion of sky for many months to come.

The gelding was quickly backed, and Telford's stable lad, 'Tommy' Woodcock, ministered to Phar Lap's needs, supplying his charge with the large quantities that a hungry youngster, destined to make nearly seventeen hands, demanded at each feed, and endeavouring with meticulous grooming and strapping and exercise to muscle up the big, ungainly frame. But the training was not a great success, as other trainers, watching Par Lap's so-called progress with undisguised scorn, were not slow to point out.

It was difficult to decide whether the horse was plain bone idle, or whether he was really unable to co-ordinate his legs properly, but the chestnut refused to work on the track and for all their faith in his potential, it was seldom that either Woodcock or Telford could persuade the horse to extend himself in a training gallop.

In these days the training might have incorporated work in one of those specially designed swimming pools that are proving so beneficial for putting muscle on a horse, and improving his general condition, without any stress on the legs. But although for many years the good effects of sea water have been known to trainers, and a 'dip' in the sea has regularly figured in the training schedule of many American and Australian race horses, Telford relied principally on a grim programme of walking and trotting Phar Lap up and down and around the local sandhills.

They first raced him as a two-year-old early in 1929, but neither that try-out nor the four succeeding attempts brought any success, and little in the way of comfort. But in his fifth effort, in a six-furlong Sydney Turf Club maiden race at Rosehill, Phar Lap won. It was not a very notable race, but there was something about the horse's running that day that encouraged the delighted Telford to try him as a stayer. And after a short respite Phar Lap was entered in the Warwick Farm Stakes over a mile.

He finished a close fourth to three good horses, and came storming home in a style that made the pundits sit up and take notice – and that brought Telford's despised animal out of obscurity to rank fourth favourite for the Australian Jockey Club Derby that takes place early in October.

Those were vintage years for Australian jockeys and there were many great names, including that of Scobie Breasley, to further their reputation for judgement and skill. To this era belonged Jim Pike, a specialist in balancing a horse, and considered by many to head the list, and Harry Telford counted the jockey amongst his friends. Pike had grown almost tired of hearing about the potential of what appeared a very discouraging horse. And the ride he had on it in the Randwick trial, where the animal seemed excessively green and clumsy, made him no keener to accede to Telford's request not to accept a ride in the Derby that year, until Phar Lap had shown what, if anything, he could do as a three-year-old. By then Jim Pike was far from being a young unknown, struggling to make his way and accepting any ride that came along. He had the established reputation, and the wins on many first-class horses to substantiate it, to be able to pick and choose, and at one stage would have laughed to scorn any suggestion that his choice would indeed fall on Telford's chestnut horse.

But only a fortnight after Phar Lap's noticeable running in the Warwick Stakes, he came second to a well-known horse in the Chelmsford Stakes over nine furlongs, and followed that up by winning the Rosehill Guineas with the greatest ease. Jim Pike needed no more persuading, and on the day of the big race rode Phar Lap down to the start, in the first of the thirty races they were to compete in together during the next two years.

Pike was tall for a jockey and, very conscious that this horse's extra and formidable propulsion came from behind the saddle, was glad that his normal method of riding gave the chestnut's loins and quarters maximum freedom from weight. He rode well up on the neck, his knees fitting in behind the hollow formed by the point of a horse's shoulder and wither, an adaptation of the familiar forward crouch introduced to Australia by the Victorians Tot Flood and James Braden, even before the American Tod Sloan's amazing success with the style brought it into general use.

Pike had only been on Phar Lap's back once before, and since he had not been riding the horse at any other work, had missed out on the invaluable opportunities that provides for getting to know one's mount. But at once he was aware of the exceptional power incorporated in that still angular frame. He was never one to make much use of the whip, but with strong wrists and good hands and using a moderately short rein, Pike was able to contain the animal's pent-up might until, calling on his own excellent sense of timing and pace, he could release it to the best effect.

Phar Lap won the 1929 Derby by three and a half lengths, in 2 minutes 31·2 seconds. As they passed the winning post his jockey first became aware of a feeling he would one day put into words, that it would come to seem almost sacrilege to ride another horse after this one. In fact this was the start of an incredible partnership that was to last two years, and in which Phar Lap and Jim Pike took twenty-seven wins, and two second placings, out of the thirty races they started together. And from that win onwards Phar Lap started favourite, or second favourite, in every remaining race of his entire career.

Sadly, even with extensive use of the sweat box, there was no hope of Jim Pike being able to get his weight anywhere near the 7 st 6 lb Phar Lap carried in the 1929 Melbourne Cup in November, and another jockey had to be given the ride. But although Phar Lap started favourite he plainly resented his new partner, playing up at the start and, after leading in the straight, was beaten into third place by four lengths. Perhaps if Phar Lap had won, Telford might have been tempted to continue racing him without much of a rest, but as it was he decided to give the horse a spell off work and away from the track.

Nothing could have been more advantageous. Three months later, when Phar Lap came up from pasture, the gangling giant had filled out and deepened into a huge, beautifully proportioned three-year-old with quarters and limbs that well advertised his speed, staying power and length of stride. And the fiery glint of his rich chestnut coat, combined with the 'presence', possessed by all great horses – and people – to earn him the press name of 'the Red Terror'.

The winnings of Harry Telford's great horse were rapidly turning his owner into a rich man, and Phar Lap himself had become the hero of the Australian public and press, but not everything was pure 'light from the sky'. By the time the chestnut was entered for the 1930 Melbourne Stakes – an autumn race that precedes the famous Melbourne Cup – he had won twenty-three times. The horse's almost unconquerable prowess on the track made it impossible for Telford to get worthwhile odds, and his fortune had to be amassed entirely from prize money. And fame was also bringing something much more sinister in its train.

The exploits and photographs of Australia's 'Wonder Horse' were continually in the news, and it was not long before they were accompanied by stories of evil attempts to nobble him. These accounts, combined with his legendary size and speed, built up Phar Lap's following to the largest ever enjoyed by any Australian racehorse, before or since, but many, including Jim Pike, dismissed the 'gangster' rumours as sensational journalese designed to keep the pot boiling. Harry Telford however was convinced there was a real danger, and had been taking what precautions he could for a long time. Wherever Phar Lap went he was accompanied by his devoted attendant, Tommy Woodcock, and no-one else was allowed to open the horse's stall. And then, only hours before Phar Lap was to run in the Melbourne Stakes, the sensed peril became only too real. As Woodcock was riding him at exercise the horse was fired at from an approaching car, the pellets smacking into a wooden fence behind them.

Fortunately Phar Lap was quite unhurt, and proved the fact by winning his race that day in a canter – a feat that shortened his odds for the Cup to 6–1 on, and increased Telford's apprehensions for his horse's safety. He decided to move Phar Lap, and three days before the race took him to a farm at Geelong, less than fifty miles from the Flemington track at Melbourne. But even then, the favourite very nearly did not make it, though the nobbler this time was a machine. On the day of the big race the horse-float carrying its precious cargo left the farm in pouring rain. Telford and Woodstock, both armed, were sitting in with the horse and there was a police escort before and behind the vehicle, but they had barely got going before the engine seized. Whether this was fate or sabotage is not known, but it took half an hour of cranking before they could get under way again, and they arrived at the track with barely half an hour to go before the start. But a bit of a rush was not going to upset Phar Lap. Like all great racehorses, he combined a sense of occasion and the heart and will to win with his physical attributes, and that day he carried Jim Pike to a three-length victory in the jockey's first Melbourne Cup.

Telford's three-year lease of the horse was due to expire in February 1931, and before that day arrived the trainer set out to ensure his capital gains. Phar Lap was raced four times in the fourteen days immediately after the Melbourne Cup, winning on each occasion, and in one week netting prize money amounting to £12,429. When the day of reckoning arrived Telford had no difficulty in paying out the agreed £4,000 to David Davis for a half share in the horse, and since Phar Lap was to win a further £20,000 in stake money in the remaining fourteen months of his life, it proved a profitable investment.

It was an over-strenuous programme, and since the physical effort of racing so frequently was combined with carrying the increasing, penalising weight, a lesser horse must surely have broken down. Phar Lap appeared to take it literally in his stride, but Jim Pike always felt that it was too much, and that one race in particular tested Phar Lap's stamina beyond the limit.

He had stormed up the Flemington track that year to take the Melbourne Cup, to the wild delight of what was a record crowd even for the race that annually brings Australia to a standstill. And he followed up by winning three more races before tackling the Victorian Amateur Turf Club Futurity Stakes, carrying 10 st 3 lb. That was a hard, bitter race to win, and Pike, the only one fully to appreciate the enormous effort required to do it, considered that Phar Lap was never quite the same again, and possibly sustained an internal strain that day. But still the races continued, still the stake money flowed in, and to public and press at least the Red Terror seemed well nigh invincible.

In 1931, when he was five, Phar Lap won seven times before successfully tackling the Melbourne Stakes for the second successive year. But then Pike did his utmost to prevent Telford and Davis from running the horse in the Melbourne Cup so soon afterwards. The jockey knew Phar Lap was not sound, he had felt the hesitation in his stride in the last yard that gave them victory, but outside pressures were to over-rule Pike's warning. At the time Australian racing was in the doldrums with the crowds growing steadily less at each meeting. That year the famous Cup was only worth £5,200, (in 1972 it was $A 103,000), a reduction born of necessity that made it the smallest prize for the event for twenty-four years. Only Phar Lap could boost the attendance, only his appearances revived the prestige of the sport. And if the Red Terror, favourite, did not line up for the Melbourne Cup that year it was not only the big money that would be lost. The thousands of Phar Lap fans, the little punters who followed the champion when and wherever he appeared to bet their last shilling on his gleaming hide, would be irretrievably let down.

David Davis had these and other cogent arguments put to him by the chairman of the Victoria Racing Club, and was left in no doubt that he owed it to the public to run his horse. He knew, too, that Telford felt no plea of unsoundness would be believed if they withdrew, at such a late hour, the hot favourite who had just added eight wins in a row to his incredible record. Phar Lap was not scratched.

He came to the start with 11 st 10 lb up. Whether the horse was indeed unsound by then is almost immaterial, because even his great heart and strength could not cope with the weight. Directly Jim Pike was convinced of this he did not try to ride the horse out and force the impossible, and the race was taken by an animal called White Nose.

Big money and racing policy are tricky matters to agree upon, and Davis and Telford were not unique in failing about this time to make their partnership work amicably. Maybe it was over general dissatisfaction with the declining purse money to be won in Australia, but obviously Harry Telford did not agree with Davis's suggested remedy. And when Davis, lured by a glittering first prize of $100,000 for the Agua Caliente Handicap at Tijuana, close inside the Mexican border, set off with Phar Lap for America, his partner was not with him and Tommy Woodcock held the status of trainer. The jockey, Billy Elliott, flew from Australia especially to take the ride.

Phar Lap's prestige preceded him to such effect that the prize money had been cut to under $21,000 dollars by the time he arrived. When he split his hoof, went lame and had to undergo an emergency operation, his owner, backing heavily, could still only get odds of 7–2 and overnight the price dropped to 6–4. The split hoof was repaired, but there was no question of galloping Phar Lap until only three days before the race, yet he lined up for the first, and as it happens only time outside Australia, hot favourite at 6–5.

Knowing too well the limitations of Phar Lap's training for the race, Tommy Woodcock, for all his faith in the horse's ability, must have felt some apprehension when he saw the chestnut running near last. Then it happened. As the crowd roared their appreciation and disbelief, Elliott brought the huge horse to the front in an incredible rush over the remaining two furlongs of the twelve involved. As they came to the last furlong post Phar Lap seemed to falter for a moment, but then swept on to pass the winning post in the record breaking time of 2 minutes 2·8 seconds.

The crowd went wild. Never had they imagined such speed, such strength, such a magnificent horse, but neither they nor anyone else were destined to see Phar Lap race again. During the succeeding prize-giving ceremony someone tried to slip a flower garland round the horse's neck for the benefit of the camera crews, and he backed away, to slip sideways off some steps. The injury to his near-fore tendon was not all that serious, but both Davis and Woodcock knew that this new mishap, coming on top of that to his hoof, meant a complete rest until his legs were again 100 per cent sound. They took Phar Lap to San Francisco to recuperate at the stables of a wealthy breeder, and a fortnight later he was dead.

He collapsed in his box and died on 5 April 1932, from what appeared to be an acute attack of colic. But then the theories and stories started to circulate, and the postmortem seemed to point to something more sinister than just colic. In Australia the rumours were bandied about that their beloved champion had been nobbled at last, poisoned by an American race gang. In America some believed that the horse had been killed by the special food brought over with him from Australia, made deadly by the heat; grass sprayed with weed killer was another suggested cause. Jim Pike, the jockey who formed the legendary partnership with the Red Terror, stuck to his idea of previous internal strain. But no-one knew for sure then, and the true cause of Phar Lap's death has never been determined. All that was certain was that one of the world's greatest racehorses was no more, and the press of three countries, New Zealand, Australia and the USA, reflected a public mood of mourning that was unprecedented.

Yet for all his thirty-seven wins out of fifty-one starts, the time records in at least four races, and total winnings of £70,121, Phar Lap was still only a horse, and in Australia there have been many other great names of the race-track to conjure with – his own fine ancestor Carbine, Shennon, the great mare Flight, the mighty Bernborough, Tulloch, Todman, Gunsynd, the names are legion. But no other animal, before or since, has captivated the public's imagination to the same extent as Phar Lap, the ugly bargain yearling that became Australia's champion horse.

II
INDIAN MAGIC

The story of Indian Magic is the tale of a dream that materialised. It began in 1878 when Wilfred and Lady Anne Blunt, two inveterate British travellers, became entranced with the beauty and endurance of pure-bred Desert Arabian horses, and at the same time were concerned at their relative rarity, even in those early days, in the Middle East. They therefore conceived the idea of starting up a stud to ensure the continuance of the breed outside its country of origin.

These are the horses that the Bedouin, the traditional horse-breeders of Arabia, term *asil*: animals of absolute blood purity, tracing back through the mares to one of the few cherished blood lines that stem from at least the seventh century, and with pedigrees that have been handed down by word of mouth and as jealously guarded as those of the Bedouin themselves. They come from a comparatively small stock of horses, isolated through the centuries from alien blood partly by the geography of the remote regions where the tribes followed the ancient grazing trails. They were culled of intent as well as by the natural order of the survival of the fittest, and in-bred and line-bred so that the innate physical differences of Arabian horses to any other breed became fixed, their characteristic beauty and intelligence, speed and hardiness, unsullied.

As centuries passed a nucleus of the pure-bred mares were still

86

kept from mating with non-pedigree horses, but through Arab invasions and subsequent trade their stallions used the remarkable potency of the Arabian horse to influence most European breeds. Less than three hundred years ago the Thoroughbred was founded on Arabian blood.

Inevitably as time passed more and more pure-bred horses were sold abroad, and soon poverty was forcing the Bedouin to be less selective in their breeding. The scarcity of pure-breds in the Middle East, noted by the Blunts at the end of the nineteenth century, has become more marked with time until, today, outside those at the Royal Jordanian Stud and a small number in other Arab countries, there are not many truly *asil* horses left in Arabia. But through the Blunts' initial efforts famous studs of well-bred Arabians have been built up in many other countries.

On later expeditions the Blunts were lucky in obtaining sufficient pure-bred horses to found their soon famous Crabbet Stud in Sussex, and with more fine stock from a celebrated Egyptian stud that was being dispersed they began another, their own Sheykh Obeyd Stud, near Cairo.

The Blunts continued with the ancient desert principles of breeding their horses strictly according to pedigree, and soon Crabbet Arabians, of different blood lines but of the same overall high standard, were of such good repute that the majority of the great studs in Britain and many other countries were founded on Crabbet stock.

When the Blunts separated in 1906 the stud was also divided, although exchanges between the two establishments continued. After 1915, when Lady Anne returned to the Egyptian stud where she eventually died, and when, back in England, her husband was soon dying also, both British studs suffered from neglect.

Eventually the Blunts' daughter, Lady Wentworth, acquired Crabbet and started on the uphill task of re-establishing its reputation. It took time and a lot of hard work, but with her whole-hearted interest in the project and an extensive knowledge of horses and their management, she achieved her objective. Soon the Crabbet horses were again being shown with much success, but there was need of some new blood to prevent too much in-breeding. And from the moment Lady Wentworth saw the ethereal beauty of a pure-white stallion that had been imported during the First World War, noted the splendidly long, curving neck, the large, low-set eyes and all the fiery elegance shown by the best of his breed, she knew that this was the horse for Crabbet.

Skowronak was Polish bred and, despite its verification, some have questioned his purity of pedigree. Possibly to a Bedouin, fanatical on the subject, this horse would not be considered truly '*asil*', but the fact remains that for generation after generation all the Skowronak stock have bred pure, stamped with the original's magnificent quality and with never a suspicion of a tainted 'throwback'. At Crabbet, Skowronak was to found a new dynasty.

One of his sons, called Naseem and sold to Russia, sired both Negative, who produced a number of quality, highly priced progeny in America, and another, sold to South Africa at the age of eighteen, named Raktha.

Of the same quality as Skowronak but with the splendid dappled markings of his grey coat making him almost more of a gem, Raktha, like his grand-sire, was one of the smaller, European-bred Arabians, of the size more typical of the desert-bred horse than those that from better feeding and a softer envirionment tended to grow bigger. For while these larger animals would be useless in their original habitat, and the small horse, admirably adapted to the desert, has evolved there through the rigours of the climate, scanty hand-feeding, and the Bedouin policy of deliberately limiting their horses' drinking, an animal with more height and substance is better suited to European and American requirements.

Lady Wentworth was fully aware of the potential market for Arabian horses over the desert-bred height, but although, in the mild climate and lush grazing of Britain the majority of those she bred grew some inches larger anyway, she was well aware of the dangers attached to breeding for more size yet. Too often height is only attained at the expense of many of the Arabian characteristics, and any faults in conformation, the poor withers and weak hocks for instance to which there is a tendency, can be accentuated in the larger animal.

But the owner of the Crabbet Stud, by then steeped in the ancient history and romance of the lovely animals she bred, had the overriding ambition to produce Arabians that retained all the beauty and individuality of their kind, yet were large horses, adapted to the world market for which she catered.

Such an aim could only be achieved through the most careful selective breeding, and that is a long-term policy, but after some years a definite Crabbet type was evolved. These, bigger than average yet true Arabians, many with the long neck of the Skowronak line, the majority with better withers than the smaller animals, found favour in most parts of the world. But Lady Wentworth's ambition went further than this, and in April 1954 her dream came true.

That was the date of birth of a colt foal, the progeny of a Crabbet mare called Indian Crown and the famous Raktha — re-bought for Crabbet some years previously — and therefore a great-grandson of the legendary Skowronak. But although she admired the lovely little head and perfect proportions of this latest addition to the Crabbet Stud, Lady Wentworth cannot then have realised that here was the animal that would materialize her dream. That this was the masterpiece of the Crabbet dynasty that would grow into a magnificent horse of 15 hands $2\frac{1}{2}$ inches, but prophetically the colt was named Indian Magic.

Grey is predominant in the Skowronak line, but as with the majority of this breeding, the foal was born chestnut like his dam. By four months he was showing the small flecks of grey round the eyes that promise a grey horse eventually, and then there was a period, the stage that many of his breeding and size go through, when he could amost have been called 'plain' and his colour was an indeterminate greyish roan.

In later years new owners were sometimes to be disappointed with young 'Magic' stock, not realsing that these horses can take eight or nine years to mature and blossom into their full beauty. But by the time Indian Magic was three he had grown into a magnificent young stallion, dappled, if without the outstanding 'rocking-horse' markings of his father, and with all the distinction that the non-colour of grey, particularly as it lightens with age, bestows. His neck, one of his best points, was even better than that of his antecedents and that and his height were exactly suited to his splendid proportions. And if the ultra critical carped that Magic was then too thick in the throat, time dealt with this, just as the years brought refinement to his head until it resembled the chiselled artistry of a Michael Angelo sculpture. He had the tapered muzzle, full, dark eyes and delicately curved, small ears of the perfect Arabian. And with it all a wonderful shoulder and length of neck, and limbs that, like his feet were hard as iron, the hocks not over-bent – that common fault amongst the breed – yet not too straight to lose the spring that is the source of the Arabian horse's unique ability to 'float' over the ground.

Magic always carried his tail like a flag, in the gay, strong carriage that the Bedouin consider should enable a good stallion to support his rider's cloak. He was always full of his own importance with a proud, magnificent bearing that, when he was already inches taller than his rivals in the show-ring made him stand out over all, sometimes to his detriment in the eyes of judges prejudiced against the large type of Arabian.

All the Crabbet horses, colts and fillies alike, and even if to be used solely for breeding, were broken as three-year-olds. True to the intelligence and co-operation of his kind, and of his line in particular, Magic proved easy to train and it was possible to back him without trouble within a fortnight.

And all through his life, although this horse's destiny was to sire animals close to his own standard of perfection, Magic was always used under saddle and provided a quiet, beautiful ride, obviously in his element and displaying the brilliant walk, dancing, floating trot and free, fast gallop that make a well-schooled Arabian the ideal hack. He was never a 'pet', as such, to be pushed around by anyone – many stallions that are quiet to ride can be difficult to lead and handle – and he was too vital, too 100 per cent alive not to show some 'temperament'. From the beginning he was a one-man horse and Fred Rice, who looked after him for so many years, had no trouble in establishing a perfect understanding with his charge. Magic was never keen on being touched by strangers, a trait that was accentuated in old age, but although he might 'shout' at a visitor taking liberties, this was done to frighten and he was never actually ill-tempered.

With his inborn alertness and high spirits Indian Magic would not have been an easy proposition for someone who was afraid of him, and he was the type that, given the chance to come to grips with another stallion, would at once have been on the defensive. Some owners of his stock, people not previously acquainted with the breed, have occasionally found themselves in difficulties, but it is a fact that while Arabian mares usually combine great gentleness with brain, the majority of the stallions mix their high intelligence with a fire that is innate and needs to be understood.

Indian Magic was never to be shown a great deal, but he won his first prize, at the Arab Horse Show at Roehampton, as a two-year-old in 1956, and included a championship at the Royal Show amongst the eight firsts he won that year. After that triumph it was almost decided to retire him from the ring, and then in 1957 Lady Wentworth died. Although many of the Crabbet horses were sold, most of those exported to carry their invaluable blood to the USA and South America, to India, Australia and the Continent, Mr Covey, who became legatee, was able to carry on with the same highly successful lines, if perforce on a smaller scale. Fortunately Indian Magic was amongst the nucleus of horses he retained, and in 1958 the stallion was again heading the line-up at Richmond and collected another championship, at Hindon, in 1962.

For years the Crabbet horses had been the Mecca for all who love and admire the Arabian breed, but from whatever land the frequent visitor hailed, whether as once occurred, it was Ibn Saud's son with his entourage from distant Saudi Arabia, or a group of wealthy industrialists from Manhatten, the horse everyone always wished to see above all others was Indian Magic, whose fame had spread around the world. And the stallion, if not exactly welcoming too close attentions, was always ready and eager, great show-man that he was, to display the spirit and zest for life that never left him until extreme old age.

At Crabbet the horses were broken and often exercised on a peat-floored, enclosed riding ring, with a little balcony for the many who came to look. Here Fred Rice had encouraged Magic's fondness for 'playing', until the stallion always put on a special 'show' for the spectators. He loved to display his fire and beauty, rearing and cavorting to order, and then demonstrated the affection he had for his handler, as well as the trust Fred Rice had in his charge, by nudging him in the back and so pushing him right across the arena.

In the days when the circus was still top-flight entertainment the horse acts were always the backbone of the show. But whether it was a 'dancing' horse with rider, displaying the skills that never quite aspired to *haute école*, or whether it was a troupe of wonderfully caparisoned Liberty Horses exhibiting breathtaking grace and beauty combined with instant obedience, all the great trainers preferred to work with Arabian stallions.

One or two of the Crabbet horses, those considered not quite up to standard, joined the Big Top, and these included a son of Indian Magic's called Mehrwan, a horse that soon proved he had inherited his sire's enjoyment for showing off.

Indian Magic liked to conclude his own private circus performance by putting his head over the fence near to his audience, there to rear up and squeal when they came closer to pay tribute. At such times he appeared a fiery, tempestuous creature, an essence of movement and vigour that it was impossible to visualise ever standing quietly or at rest. Yet the horse loved children and was very gentle with them, and for years his constant and cherished companion was a cat, Freddie, that shared his box. True on one occasion, in a moment of over-rough horse-play, Magic picked up his furry friend and dropped him out in the yard, but Freddie seemed not to mind and had soon returned to egg on the stallion by standing up and 'boxing' him with his paws. Most days the cat was to be seen sitting in a contented hump on the top of Magic's half-door, or else curled up asleep sharing his straw bed.

Like most of his breed Indian Magic was long lived and in 1970, at Kempton Park, when he proudly led a parade of Arabian champions and personalities of past years, there was little about his looks to show he was then twenty-seven years old. But then, not long after, when Indian Magic did at last start to go down-hill, Mr Covey humanely saved his favourite from further deterioration by having him put down. This was in 1972, and for months after Magic's death Freddie the cat, by then himself a venerable seventeen year old, roamed the stables looking for his friend. But although his quest could never be realised, Indian Magic and much of his magnificence lives on in his progeny. He sired a great number of lovely animals, amongst them Silver Moonlight, one of the earliest, that was sold to

Australia where he became a leading sire, and then continued his breeding career at the age of twenty when he was re-exported to the USA. Silver Magic, a full sister, went to Australia, too, and another grey son, Touch of Magic, who was a notable jumper, also proved a breeder of excellent stock in America.

Many of Magic's progeny are producing stock of the type much sought after nowadays, both abroad and in Britain where the breed is now better appreciated and is growing in popularity. For although as far back as the early '20s the Arab Horse Society was holding shows and organising long-distance tests — and the excellence of the part-Arab, particularly in show-hack and show pony classes in this country has been more than proved — the pure-bred Arabians were for a long while only of real interest to the already converted. There was a lengthy interlude when they were commonly seen only, shown 'in hand', at a few of the larger shows, often far too fat to do justice to their innately lovely proportions, and looked on by the majority as creatures of impracticable beauty and little every day use.

A Fifty Mile Ride at Goodwood some years ago well illustrated Arabian endurance, and nowadays Arabian horses and those with Arab blood often dominate such arduous contests as the Golden Horse-Shoe Ride. Half-breds and Anglo-Arabs are seen competing at more Horse Trials and Dressage Competitions, and at least one annual One Day Event is held for Arabian horses only. And while few of the breed could, or would be expected to emulate Senrab, the little registered Arabian gelding that was habitually clearing six feet in America in the '50s, the myth that these horses cannot jump has long been disproved.

Of all Indian Magic's offspring his grey son, Scindian Magic, a 15.2 hand champion in his own right, is one of the best. He gets wonderful pure breds, but is most noted for the quality of the Anglo-Arabs he sires. These are the perfect answer for those who want a horse larger than the Arabian and that combines its attributes with that of a Thoroughbred. In France the Anglo-Arab has long been an important part of the riding scene, and is used for racing — particularly steeplechasing, show-jumping, dressage, eventing and hunting. In that country it is produced from an admixture of Arab blood (a minimum of twenty-five per cent) and Thoroughbred to native stock, and unlike British Anglo-Arabs, which are a constantly repeated fifty-fifty Arabian/Thoroughbred cross, the French version is used for reproduction of its own kind.

The beautiful pure-breds and Anglo-Arabs sired by Scindian Magic are yet another of the many branches of the famous line, now represented in many countries of the world, to lead back to Indian Magic – that dream of a horse that came true.

12
FOXHUNTER

Until the enclosure of common land at the beginning of the eighteenth century, the riders disporting themselves in pursuit of deer or fox had been able to hunt with small need for a man and his horse to do anything but gallop gaily where they would. Then the Enclosure Act of 1709, passed by Parliament to increase food production, parcelled up the majority of heaths and commons, and the consequent private owners made their boundaries plain with the aid of hedges and fences that changed the face of rural England. If the national sport was to continue then riders must teach their horses to jump, and learn to stay with them when they did. And surprisingly, since nature did not really design a horse for anything much in the way of leaping, the animals not only proved willing but efficient, as Xenophon discovered more than twenty-five centuries ago.

Jumping, other than as a means to an end and as the merest glimmer of show-jumping as we know it today, began with one class embodied in a Paris harness show in 1866. Three jumping classes were included in the 1900 Olympic Games, and by the 1912 Olympics there were both team and individual show jumping events.

In England the beginning of the century saw a few 'lepping' competitions, dull affairs with the only obstacle a single rail that was raised after each round, and even in the years immediately prior to the first World War a 'course' usually consisted of only four fences. When international competitions began to get going the British were characteristically slow to adopt the 'new fangled' forward seat, introduced and perfected by the great Italian horseman Caprilli, and were sadly, and literally left behind. Between 1918 and 1930 the number of fences was increased to seven, but they were all of the 'straight up' variety, and up to the Second World War the courses were designed for very slow, very boring precision jumping.

After the Second World War, when the sport got going again in 1945 largely owing to the inspiration of Lieutenant Colonel 'Mike' Ansell and his small band of like-thinking enthusiasts, courses, fences and competitions were entirely re-designed. Riders and horses alike required more courage and better balance, and in the case of the horses more freedom as well, in order to tackle the varied fences that included big spreads. The result of the changes presented a new challenge to riders, new interest and excitement for spectators, and soon the speed and scope required called for a new type of show-jumper, usually with Thoroughbred blood and very different from the slow, common animals that were found most suitable before. The new conditions were exactly suited to the type and capabilities of a horse called Foxhunter.

This bay horse was foaled in 1940 and was by the Thoroughbred sire, Erehwemos, — a name arrived at by reversing the word 'somewhere' – that belonged to the Duke of Westminster. His dam, Catcall, was a hunter bred by a steeplechaser, and her grand-dam had been a pure-bred Clydesdale.

Foxhunter spent the first years of his life in Norfolk, on the farm of his owner, a Mr Millard, and from the earliest days showed a friendly trust in humans, and the innate ability to jump any little hazard he came across — a pastime he indulged in and enjoyed. At three years old he was sold for £60, a sum nowadays that would barely acquire the smallest, most unpretentious pony, and was taken to live in the famous hunting county of Leicestershire.

Foxhunter was by then a big and powerful horse standing 16.3 hands, but he possessed such a calm, co-operative temperament that breaking-in presented few problems, and it was not long before he received his first introduction to hounds. Well before this it had become obvious that the jumping potential of his early days would be fulfilled, and in the free-for-all of two seasons in the hunting field, Foxhunter acquired the ability to look after himself and get out of trouble that was to make him such a reliable, safe as well as a brilliant show-jumper.

With a horse like this the step from hunting to show-jumping was an obvious one, but the transition was not unduly hurried. A show-jumper has to be obedient and immediately responsive to its rider if it is to achieve the higher grades, and it must also be physically and mentally mature to give of its best. It says much for Foxhunter's talent that without being unduly pushed he hit the headlines as a six-year-old, at the time the youngest horse in the history of show-jumping to get into the top flight, and caught the attention of Lieut. Colonel Harry Llewellyn, who was to prove himself the greatest exponent of show-jumping we have yet seen.

Colonel Llewellyn and Foxhunter began their renowned partnership in 1947. It usually takes rider and horse some while to combine sufficiently to start winning in the ring, but these two, the outstanding rider with an equally talented horse, came to an understanding so quickly that their successes in that first season ensured them a place in the team representing Great Britain at international shows in Ostend, Blackpool and Newport.

That year Britain began to appear on the international show jumping scene more than ever before, and this helped to popularise the sport with the general public. It also meant that Foxhunter and the other British horses and their riders had to adapt their style of jumping from that suited to shows held under British Show Jumping Rules, to those run according to the Féderation Equestre Internationale. When Foxhunter was gaining purely British experience in a show, he would be required to canter slowly between the obstacles before being carefully 'placed' for the take-off by Colonel Llewellyn. When he made his first appearance at the White City for the Royal International Horse Show that year, and competed for the King George v Cup, an individual award that he was to win the next year, and in 1950 and again in '53, he was competing under FEI rules. At that time the method of calculating faults at each fence was dissimilar to that used by the BSJA, but the main difference was that 'time' was (as it still is) the deciding factor – and this meant that Foxhunter had to learn to go much faster, at a cadenced gallop between the obstacles, to avoid being penalised. This meant also being able to 'place' himself to a greater extent, with less dependence on his rider, a jumping method for which the days following hounds across country had been excellent preparation.

The BSJA, the governing body of show jumping in Britain, were anxious that the top-flight British horses should get as much experience of international jumping as possible, because 1948 was an Olympic year, with the contests to be staged at Wembley Stadium. And based on the results of these events a nucleus of top-class horses and riders, including Colonel Llewellyn and Foxhunter, were chosen to train as 'possibles' for the British team.

In those days the British show-jumpers had few of the facilities for training enjoyed by their rivals abroad, and with only a relatively short preparation the team came to Wembley to do battle with the other nations who had sent the pick of their horses and riders to England that year. The course was big and testing but very fair, and the chief hazard was the going, muddy and deep, that got progressively worse. By the time Foxhunter came into the arena, for the third round of the competition, the ground was really treacherous. There had been many refusals and three countries had been eliminated. Foxhunter did well to get round with sixteen faults, to take equal seventh place with his team-mate Kilgeddin and a French horse, and to give Great Britain a creditable third place in the Grand Prix des Nations.

In the next, the 1950 season, Colonel Llewellyn and Foxhunter continued to distinguish themselves at home, and were established as the most outstanding partnership then show-jumping in Europe. With the British team they set off in June to compete at the official Concours Hippique. They came to Lucerne, with its fine showground down by the lake that includes five natural banks, three water jumps, the permanent, neatly clipped bush fences and solid stone walls. There Foxhunter put up a magnificent performance to win the Prix du Burgenstock, and the Grand Prix de la Ville de Lucerne. His two clear rounds in the Nations' Cup gained him the best individual prize in that competition, and were a major factor in

Britain's victory over from Switzerland, France, Ireland, Italy and Chile.

At Vichy, Britain lost the Prix des Nations to France, but Foxhunter took the Prix de la Compagnie Fermière; a puissance (high jump) progressive, after a series of exciting barrages; was second in the Prix des Vainqueurs, and had two other thirds. His wonderful jumping at the White City then gave him the George v Gold Challenge Cup for the second time, and the Moss Bros. Cup, and his two clears, with the same by Nizefela and Red Star, in the Prince of Wales Cup assured Britain of retaining it. In Dublin Foxhunter's proven brilliance over any type of course aided Britain to carry off the Aga Khan Trophy. He wound up the season this side of the Atlantic by winning the Beaufort Stakes at the Horse of the Year Show at Harringay, and the FEI Competition over two courses, victories that, added to a first with Silver Queen in the Pair Relay Competition, gave Colonel Llewellyn the coveted Harringay Spurs.

By now Foxhunter's name was a household word in Britain, and his benign, intelligent face was as familiar as that of the era's film stars. That autumn he and Colonel Llewellyn went off with the team on a restricted tour of America and Canada, and competed in Harrisburgh, New York, and Toronto, where Foxhunter added to other honours by collecting the trophy for the International Broad Jump at the Royal Fair. On this tour he also built up an additional fan club on the other side of the Atlantic, comparable in size to that awaiting him at home.

They opened the 1951 international season in springtime, at Nice. Then it was: Prix de Monaco, puissance – 1st . . . Foxhunter; Prix Bucephale – 3rd . . . Foxhunter; Prix des Nations – 2nd . . . Great Britain. On to Rome, to the Piazza di Siena in the Borghesi Gardens where the arena, set amongst cypress and umbrella pines, is one of the most beautiful in the world and where the courses, with their doubles and trebles placed at awkward distances and the light fences constructed from birch poles that are difficult to see, were some of the most testing. And there it was: Premio Palatino – 1st . . . Foxhunter; Premio Campidoglio (puissance) – 2nd . . . Foxhunter; Premio delle Naxioni (Nations' Cup) – 2nd . . . Great Britain, tied with France. They took a second and a third, and another second with Mrs. Llewellyn riding, in the outdoor arena in Madrid, where it takes a bold horse to cope with the large spreads. Then it was back for the International Horse Show in London, to collect the Welcome Stakes, the White City Stadium Cup, the Daily Mail Cup, a second in the King George v Cup, and a combined effort with the team-mates Nizefela, Aherlow, and Red Star II, to win the Prince of Wales Cup.

In Dublin the score was two firsts in addition to the team event; in Ostend, two firsts and a third. Le Zoute produced only two seconds, and a second for the team in the Prix des Nations – but Foxhunter won the Individual in that competition. So they came again to the Horse of the Year Show to win the Fred Foster Memorial Competition, a second in the Daily Graphic Cup, and a third in the Beaufort Stakes. They were in trouble at Geneva at the bank, resulting in a rib injury for Colonel Llewellyn, but that was the only set-back and the year had been good preparation for Helsinki and the next Olympics.

Foxhunter and the other horses on the short list had earned a good rest and were given it in the winter of '51. Then there were two months of slow work to get them into trim before going to Aldershot, at the beginning of April, to start serious training. Based on performance during the past season and sometimes changed, perforce, owing to injury to horse or rider, the team had been whittled down to Colonel Llewellyn, team captain, riding Foxhunter; Wilf White with his splendid ex-plough horse, Nizefela; and Lieut. Colonel Duggie Stewart on the loaned mare, Aherlow, with several other horses in reserve.

The preparation for any Olympic event is a gruelling one, and there were long hours of tough training when riders gained invaluable experience in riding their horses under conditions similar to those they would encounter. But apart from this the competative jumping must go on, and without giving the horses too hard a season a tour was arranged where the different members of the team jumped at a few shows chosen with care, where the courses were just what was needed and the results very satisfactory. They came together again for more training practices over small courses at a couple of shows, then remained at Aldershot until the ground became dangerously hard. On 26 July a final training practice at Windsor was watched by the Queen.

On 31 July the papers were carrying new photographs of Foxhunter, taken the previous day. Over the years the public had come to expect frequent pictures of their favourite, jumping every type of obstacle in competitions all over the world, standing by while his owner received a 'Foxhunter' statuette from the Queen, being patted by Princess Margaret, or at home in his stable yard, but this was something quite new. These studies showed Foxhunter, rugged up and wearing knee-pads, and sporting the curved head pad fixed behind his ears, *de rigueur* for a horse about to embark in an aeroplane. It was the first time he or any of the horses had flown, but there were no problems on the five-and-a-half hour flight to Helsinki, and they arrived fitter than those of any other team, and ready to face the great test in the Olympic Stadium on 3 August.

The course for that great day had problems such as the double, parallel bars with a double oxer about 29 foot away, that needed to be taken at speed with only one non-jumping stride between. The water was big, 16 or 17 foot, followed quickly by a 5 foot 4 inch gate, but the overall impression was of a not too difficult course, and one that was very fair — but large enough for horses jumping for the first time in a totally unfamiliar venue.

British hopes were high, both within the team and with the many supporters round the huge arena, not to mention the tens of thousands back home who waited with confidence to see their champion horse and his worthy team-mates bring home the gold for Britain.

Nizefela went first, to jump a superb round with only the gate down for four faults. The less dependable Aherlow did very well for twelve faults. The British total — sixteen, and Foxhunter to come.

This was the horse that was even then undoubtedly the greatest show-jumper of his or any subsequent generation, with the proud record, apart from the occasional foot in the water, of not hitting a fence in his last nine consecutive Nations Cups. He was racehorse fit and better muscled up than he had ever been, but so that he should not be tired for the second round he had not been given as much work as usual that morning. And so, instead of the calm, obedient partner which the Colonel had come to expect, he found himself coping with a Foxhunter bursting out of his skin with good spirits, but sadly inattentive to the vital matters in hand. The big horse came into the huge, flag-bedecked arena gazing about him at the crowds and the colours, and fully prepared to shy at the fences. He was disobedient when asked to lengthen his stride, and fought against coming back to his rider's hand when required. The Colonel dared not risk telling his horse to jump off a long stride or stand off his fences, and had to check him back to the bottom of each obstacle. They had three fences down, and with a circle at the wall when, owing to Foxhunter's antics, his rider nearly fell off, clocked up an unbelievable, for them, sixteen and three-quarters faults – on the one occasion when it mattered most.

But a lot of work was put in before that second round, and Foxhunter came to the second phase in a very different frame of mind. Supremely confident and in tune with his rider, he jumped a copybook clean round to give the British team the winning total of forty and three quarters faults, and a well-deserved proud return home with the coveted Gold Medal.

Foxhunter was semi-retired in 1953, and bowed himself out in 1956 after winning the final Committee Trophy at Dublin. In his career he represented Great Britain thirty-five times, with seventy-one International wins to his credit, and is the only horse to have won the classic King George v Gold Cup three times. There has never been another like him, and even if generations grow up who are not told the story of this famous horse his name will never be forgotten. For it was given to the competitions, designed to introduce promising novice horses to the great sport of high-level show-jumping. And many of those animals that have become famous in the flesh and on the TV screen, have indeed come to the top via the Foxhunter Jumping Competitions that culminate, for the qualified, in the exciting Foxhunter Championship held each October at the Horse of the Year Show.

13
DOUBLET

'After God, we owed the victory to horses . . .'

The writer, Hernal Diaz, was a companion of Cortez who landed with him in Mexico in 1518, and he refers to the victory over the Indian inhabitants whose land it was. The horses were eighteen of those few bred by the Spaniards in the West Indies, from animals that had managed to survive the ghastly, two-month voyage out from Spain.

They were proud, plump little horses with arched necks and flowing manes and tails, descendants of a breed, reared on the plains of Cordova, that had evolved from Moorish stallions imported from North Africa and local Spanish mares. They were the first horses to set hoof on the American continent since the Ice Age, and they and their progeny carried the conquerors over the mountains and marshes, across great rivers and through the forests of a vast, alien land. The horses assured the initial easy victories over the red men because the Indians were terror-stricken at sight of these unknown monsters. When fright turned to admiration and covetousness, horses were both stolen and traded and some of them escaped. In the wild they bred and prospered and formed eventually the huge herds of *mesteño*, feral horses, the mustangs that with the years lost the looks of their Andalusian ancestry, but gained a heritage of incredible stamina and the high intelligence born of a fight for survival.

Through the years the herds moved north and west across the continent, and many mustangs were caught by the early settlers to become the original cowponies. But gradually, in North America, the old mustang blood was bred out in favour of that of imported breeds.

In some South American countries, however, the mustang strain was preserved, particularly in the Argentine where a breeding stock of the old sturdy type was gathered from remote regions, to evolve into that admirable, now registered breed, the Criollo.

Criollos are working cattle horses second to none, their legendary stamina perpetuated by Mancha and Gato, the two of their kind that travelled with Professor Tschiffely, for two years, over the 10,000 miles from Buenos Aires to Washington.

When polo, first taught to the British in 1889 by the Nawabs of Kashmir, became popular outside Britain, in Argentina the Criollo, as a cattle pony innately handy and quick on the turn, was the obvious and ready-made mount. When the height limit for ponies was abolished and the game speeded up, the Criollos bred for polo were crossed with imported Thoroughbred sires, until what is virtually a distinct breed of Argentine polo pony has been evolved.

The fame of these ponies is world wide, and from after the war, when Prince Phillip took up the game, until he gave it up in 1971, his string always included Argentine animals, and a number of favourite mares, as they were retired, went to Sandringham to further the Queen's interests in horse breeding.

It was the Queen's ambition to breed suitable polo ponies for her husband and, later, also for her son to play, but unfortunately she had little luck with this aspect of her hobby. Usually the home-bred ponies proved incompatible, or as Prince Phillip teasingly suggests, the Queen's horses are too well fed, and some prospective polo ponies grew too big.

In 1963 Suerte, one of the most favoured of the Argentine mares, had a colt foal by Doubtless II, an Argentine-bred Thoroughbred that had raced in England. There were high hopes that this breeding really would produce a good pony for Prince Philip, but by the time the colt had grown into a handsome chestnut yearling it was obvious

that this was going to be yet another 'outsize'.

They called him Doublet, and for five years his future remained uncertain. At nearly 16.2 hands there was no question of polo, and although his full sister Effingham became one of the Queen's favourite riding horses, Doublet's temperament did not seem suited to a hack. He had not been easy to break, and although, at nearly six years old he had settled to some extent, he could still be a difficult customer to cope with. But there was potential and there were signs of jumping ability, he had the size and quality, plus the stamina of his ancestry, for an Event horse.

It was decided to send Doublet to Alison Oliver who helps Princess Anne with her Eventing ambitions, and keeps her horses at Brookfield Farm, the Oliver's stables in Berkshire.

Doublet immediately found favour in Mrs Oliver's eyes. He appeared to be highly sensitive and individualistic and still shadowed by the troubles of his youth, but she was sure he had great possibilities, and felt him to be just the type of horse the Princess needed at that stage of her riding career.

When the moment came for Princess Anne to put this theory to the test, she herself was far from sure. She was thoroughly enjoying the successful training and competing, still at novice level with her other two horses, the lively, versatile little Purple Star and a reliable Thoroughbred called Royal Ocean, but the first schooling sessions with Doublet left much to be desired. Horse and rider just did not seem to be on a wave-length, and the Princess began to doubt if they ever would be. But she has great faith in her trainer's judgement, and a challenge is always something to be taken up, so she set about adapting herself and her riding to the horse, and finding the key to his disposition.

Before very long and with the help and enthusiasm of Mrs Oliver, Doublet and his new rider were starting to come to terms. The horse was more settled and reliable, his ability became daily more apparent, and the Princess began to find what her trainer believed – that if this was a very demanding horse, equally he was a very rewarding one.

When Princess Anne first arrived at Brookfield she already possessed enormous enthusiasm for her chosen sport, the determination to work hard and the guts to take what comes in what is a very tough form of competing. She had been well taught when young, and has anyway an innate ability, plus a natural balance and rhythm to her riding. From the Queen she inherits an instinctive rapport with horses that once over the initial difficulties helped her and Doublet to form a real partnership, and from her father the fixed resolve to go in and win that inspired confidence also in her horse. But riding, particularly at the higher levels, is a very exacting sport and there is literally no end to what there is to learn. Despite the assets, in those early stages Princess Anne, in common with Doublet, had a long way to go. Once horse and rider started to understand one another, the hours of training became absorbing advances towards what was then a seemingly far off but very definite goal – Badminton, after the Olympics the toughest competition in Three Day Eventing.

Because of her public commitments Anne is never able to give the amount of time to her horses that other top-class competitors consider a 'must'. But although Alison Oliver does a great deal towards getting them fit and carries on their training programme when the Princess cannot, if Anne is within possible reach of Brookfield, she fits in several hours of hard work with Doublet and her other horses before dashing off to a royal engagement.

Sometimes she manages to do this every day for a week or so, then she may have to fly abroad on a royal tour, but there was no wasting time when she could be with Doublet. She is well aware that success in Eventing, or any other form of competing with a horse, is impossible without mutual understanding, and a great deal of concentrated training together was necessary to achieve the speed with which the Princess and Doublet made the top of the Eventing world.

The first public appearance together was on 26 June 1969, when they won a Dressage competition at Basingstoke. Responsive, full of impulsion and fluid in his movements, Doublet was proving a 'natural' at that graduated system of horse training, that should result in 'the harmonious development of the physique and ability of the horse'. And a win first time out in a competition where calmness is essential, also proved that, unlike Colombus, the difficult young 'giant' that Anne was soon to add to her string, Doublet did not 'boil up' under the emotional stresses of a crowd.

The next outing, a month later, was at Osberton. It was Doublet's first Horse Trial as such, and it says a lot for the ground work back home, and the budding partnership between rider and horse, that they won the Novice Class, and with it qualified for the Midland Bank Novice Championships at Chatsworth, where they came a creditable sixth in the following autumn.

Anne had been competing with her other horses all through that season and both Purple Star and Royal Ocean were upgraded to Intermediate early in the year, with Doublet following suit by the autumn. There had been a fair share of bad luck as well as of success, there had been the inevitable falls and 'off' days, and Anne was learning to take whatever fortune the day might bring as an accepted part of life with horses. She had also gained the satisfaction of being accepted entirely on merit by her fellow competitors.

Doublet was showing as much talent for jumping as he had for dressage. Much of the schooling of an Event horse, or of a show jumper, takes place on the ground, and there were still long hours hard at work on the soft tan of the indoor school at Brookfield, suppling up, practising different movements and imbibing the co-operative obedience essential to success. Actual jumping experience varied from popping over the rails in and out of the home paddock or dealing with the big sleeper-faced bank near the stabling, to an hour of concentrated schooling over fences in the jumping field. Even then the sessions always began with work on the ground to ensure the horse being both active and relaxed, followed by practice in correct approach and take-off over comparatively low fences, with the Princess relying on Alison Oliver's helpful criticisms and suggestions, and meticulous eye for spotting what is wrong. Exercise, fitness, and the variety that keeps a horse from getting bored, were obtained in the pleasant surroundings of nearby Warfield Park, and Doublet learned to tackle the bigger obstacles in the competitions where he was also acquiring his experience.

For a long while the Princess and her riding, and supposed ambitions, had been receiving the attentions of the press, and by then Doublet's name was appearing as well. Publicity, over-enthusiasm of the public and the horse-distracting presence of followers and photographers pressing towards a fence, are additional hazards of Anne's eventing, only encountered by other competitors to a very limited degree. As speculation grew stronger – was Princess Anne to be the first member of the royal family to ride at Badminton? Was she good enough? Was Doublet really capable of it? Would her family allow her to? – The pressures increased. The truth, that if the Princess and Doublet, both admittedly inexperienced, were not ready for Badminton '71 they would not compete, seemed to dawn on few.

Badminton had in fact been Anne's objective, however nebulous a one, ever since she and Purple Star came a satisfactory eighth in their first adult Horse Trial at Windsor in the spring of '68. But an objective does not necessarily become an achievement, and for all this rider's obvious ability, only she and her trainer were, in the earliest days, nursing the secret conviction that Badminton, with Doublet's help, would before long become a real possibility. Without him, a suitable horse would have been the big problem, for Royal Ocean was retired at the end of '69, and for all Purple Star's proven aptitude, that upgraded him to Open in the following year, he was really too small a horse for his rider to tackle the Badminton fences.

But Doublet was there, and he too had become an 'Open' horse in 1970. He had in fact qualified for Badminton that year, and it was perhaps fortunate that the Princess was on a royal tour of Australasia at the time, and therefore not tempted to have a go without an additional and invaluable year's experience. By the time the decision to enter for Badminton in 1971 had been made public, Doublet had competed at, and usually gained at least a place in a number of one day Horse Trials, and his familiarity with the show jumping phase of an event, had been increased by the occasional Foxhunter and other jumping classes. Prior to Badminton Anne managed to ring the changes by riding him to take second place in the Novice Dressage Championships at Stoneleigh, followed by a fourth in the Medium Class, and they were in the money soon after at an indoor jumping show. Doublet, gay, alert, and extra intelligent, took it all in his stride, and in early April at Rushall, considered as the 'school' for Badminton later in the month, he was unpressed to finish fourth.

Discounting the Olympics or European Championships, Badminton is considered the acme of the eventing scene. It takes place over four days, and in '71 it was held from April 22–5, and since that was a pre-Olympic year, the course was at its most severe. The competition consists of a Dressage test, where good marks can, but do not always have a bearing on the final results; then a gruelling phase of endurance, comprising many miles of roads and tracks, with a steeplechase sandwiched between, and a stiff and lengthy cross-country course to follow. In conclusion there is a show jumping phase, designed to demonstrate horse and rider's fitness and versatility after the rigorous second phase. As with any Three Day Event Badminton is a very different type of competition from a one day Horse Trial, calling for much greater courage, skill and stamina from both horse and rider, and often for a different type of horse with considerably more quality.

Princess Anne and Doublet had had the smallest taste of a Three Day Event by competing in a Two-Day affair, but otherwise they came to Badminton with only the experience of two seasons of one day Horse Trials behind them. The general opinion was that it would be good going if they were to get round.

There were competitors from Sweden, Ireland, Switzerland and Holland, and the British Opposition alone was formidable. Mary Gordon-Watson with Cornishman was there, the holders of the Individual World and European Championships; Richard Meade, that very experienced rider; Mark Philips and Great Ovation, Debbie West and Baccaret and all the other top-notch Eventing fraternity.

By the end of the Dressage the Princess and Doublet were lying second with 82·5 penalty points. The general verdict? 'Jolly good — and it would be marvellous if they could only get round the cross-country!' Anne is fully aware that a rider needs to be as fit as the horse, and she matched Doublet's stamina over the miles of roads and tracks. On the steeplechase course she contrived what is not an easy matter, particularly with a bold horse, to gauge the timing so that she could conserve his strength yet only acquire 32·0 time penalties in the process. Then it was on to the four miles, plus, of cross-country with its thirty-three solid fences.

Kept to the energy conserving rhythm of a steady gallop between obstacles, the combination of his own courage with Anne's determined riding, gave Doublet the security and confidence to take-off and meet each fence just right. There were no troubles at Number

Three, that perennial Badminton bugbear the Coffin, nor at the 4 foot 10 inch Double Oxer that follows. At Number Thirteen there was no question of trying to gallop through the thirteen foot of water as though it were just another puddle, the treatment that brought near disaster to more than one horse that day. He left a foot behind and pecked on landing over the complex of ditch and rails called the Vicarage Dee, but there were no problems with the Vicarage Ditch or the Parallel Pen, and no hesitation in jumping down into the lake in front of the big house, then splashing through and jumping out up over a 3 foot 11 inch sleeper-bank and rail. They took Number Twenty-one, the notorious Normandy Bank with just the controlled impulsion and dash required, and dealt in the same manner with the spectacular Ski Jump. Soon there were only three to go, then two, then a leap over Thirty-three, the Whitbread Bar, and on to the welcome finishing post. That added up to no jumping penalties, a mere thirty-two for time, and fourth place for Princess Anne and Doublet at the end of the day.

By the time they entered the ring the next day, for the last phase over an eleven-fence show jumping course, the emotional pressures were as big as the crowd of spectators that were generating them. As might be expected this affected both horse and rider to a degree, and Doublet appeared tensed up and a little stiff, jumping without quite his usual fluidity. He left a foot in the water, and that cost them ten penalties, and a drop of one place overall. But what a triumphant result it was, to come fifth out of forty-eight at Badminton, in a first attempt at a Three Day Event.

After Badminton, while growing speculation concentrated on whether Princess Anne and Doublet would be invited to compete in the European Three Day Championship at Burghley that autumn, the horse was given a rest until June. Meanwhile the Princess turned her attention to schooling and competing with her two young greys, a task she was finding interesting and instructive, but not easy after the satisfying partnership with Doublet – by then a mature horse ready to settle to each phase of an event as required, and with which she had a total and rewarding mutual confidence.

By the time Doublet was in work once more Burghley was still an uncertainty, but this made no difference to the programme for getting him fit. It was in full swing and Princess Anne had just been invited to compete, as an individual, in the European Championships, when illness struck and she was whisked off to hospital for an operation.

Alison Oliver continued with Doublet's training, but really there seemed no chance of anyone who had had a major operation six weeks before, being fit enough to compete in the most gruelling of all horse competitions bar the Olympics, not to mention the 'trial' event at Eridge that precedes it by some weeks. But Anne called on her reserves of youth and determination, and by sheer guts she and Doublet made both dates. Despite a fall at Eridge they were able to put up a convincing display of ability and physical fitness, and on 2 September, against all probability, they were at Burghley ready to take on an opposition that included six former Olympic riders amongst the top Eventers from eight different countries.

At Burghley, as a rough estimate, there were about eighteen miles to be ridden at varying speeds, made up of roads and tracks and the steeplechase and cross-country courses, and a total of forty-three fences to be jumped, of different kinds, but all solid and formidable. To cope with such a task Doublet needed to be so physically fit that he was almost bursting out of his skin with good spirits and well-being. It says therefore a great deal for his schooling and co-operative obedience that his calmness allied to impulsion, his cadence and lightness combined with the overall impression of 'doing it all on his own', gave him and his rider a final Dressage score of only 41·5 penalty points, 7·5 better than the runner-up, and in the enviable position of leading the field at the end of the first phase.

Despite that recent operation the Princess had no troubles with the roads and tracks, and this time perfected her speed estimate on the steeplechase course to finish without penalty. As at Badminton, there were thirty-three fences to cope with on the four mile, 1,324 yard cross country, and the combination of obstacles, each providing a different type of challenge, with the tight time limit, made it the testing championship course it proved to be.

It was a joy to watch Anne and Doublet, sharing their mutual confidence, to meet and clear thirty-two of the fences without fault. And at Number Twenty-seven, the Trout Hatchery, and the only one to cause anxiety, when Doublet slipped almost onto his stomach coming up out of the water, his rider sat tight to give him the rein to recover himself, before a reassuring pat as they went off again in the cadence of their gallop. They came in with only 18·8 penalties, for time, and took the lead at the end of phase two, 17·8 points ahead.

The pressures before the show jumping must have been much greater than at Badminton, but this time stress was not going to be allowed to affect Doublet's performance. He never looked like touching a fence, and the clear round that made him and Princess Anne the well-deserved Individual European Champions of 1971, brought a great roar of applause that set the chestnut alight as he galloped the victory circuit of the ring. For the Queen and Prince Philip, delighted spectators all through, it brought the double pleasure of a winning daughter, and a winning, home-bred horse, that the Queen had given Princess Anne for her own after the success at Badminton.

After it was all over, it was found that Doublet, like most of the other horses jumping that cross-country course, must have rapped himself on one of the fences, but the small lump, discovered on his foreleg, that showed a bruised tendon, seemed of little moment. And while the headlines concerning him and Princess Anne being selected for the Olympic team in the following year, were being firmly kept in perspective by his always realistic rider, Doublet was turned out once more for an even better deserved rest.

After nearly three months it was time to start getting him fit once more for Badminton '72, and on the result of that competition would depend any hopes, or otherwise, of being considered for inclusion in the team to represent Great Britain in the Olympics at Munich. The slight thickening on the chestnut's tendon, a leftover from the bruise, had not disappeared with rest as expected, but it did not seem to affect him in any way during the long, hard preparation. At the same time its presence did produce the tiniest niggle of doubt about his soundness, and this was something that just *had* to be resolved before a public appearance in a tough competition at Badminton. Although the leg never 'filled' or gave any pain, and produced not the slightest trouble at a one day Horse Trial at Crookham towards the end of March, that did not prove that the tendon would necessarily stand up to galloping and jumping over a near five mile course. So Doublet was given a stiff work-out on the downs near Newbury about a week beforehand – the leg did not stand up to it and he went lame.

For Princess Anne it was a terrible, if not totally unexpected disappointment and put paid to any chance of her achieving her dearest ambition, inclusion in the team for Munich. But she is not one to cry over spilt milk, and she was soon accepting it as 'just one of those things' and working hard with her younger horses.

For Doublet it meant treatment, and then being out at grass until January of 1973 when he began to work again. He did very little in the spring because of the hardness of the ground but on his first public outing, a one day Horse Trial on 7 May which was meant merely to get him used to competing again, he exceeded all expectation and finished third. Four days later, at the Spillers Combined Competition (Dressage and showjumping) at the Royal Windsor Horse Show he confirmed his apparent recovery by winning. Another good horse, Goodwill, was brought in the autumn of '72. A showjumper by trade, he was upgraded in Eventing from Novice to Open before the season finished. He came eighth at Badminton this year and may be the Princess's choice for Burghley in the autumn. If the Princess were chosen for the British team at Kiev she could ride either Doublet or Goodwill in team events, but to defend her European Individual title she must ride Doublet, the horse on which she won. If his leg remains sound then the odds are on it's being Doublet anyway that goes with his rider to Russia.

In the future, encroaching years must finally alter the position of this horse once destined to be a polo pony. But until age or unsoundness preclude him, the tribute Princess Anne paid him after Burghley in 1971 still holds good – 'there is no other one . . .'.

14
LOCHINVAR

Some years before this particular young Lochinvar came out of the west – that is from Ireland to Major and Mrs Allhusen's home in Norfolk – the initial thread of his story was already being woven by a mare called Laurien. And since Lochinvar's retirement the thread has been picked up again and woven on, like his own, spun in gold, by another famous horse called Laurieston.

These are the Allhusen's celebrated trio of event horses that have encompassed their owners' lives for many years, and from Laurien stemmed the growing interest and knowledge, the frequent successes and inevitable misfortunes in a demanding sport, that were then extended by Lochinvar, and still continue in very good measure with Laurieston.

Laurien was the daughter of a German Army transport horse, similar in type to the 'good old Irish draught mare', that, lacking a distinguishing German breed brand, hailed probably from Czechoslovakia or Poland. During the Second World War all the transport of the thirty German divisions in Italy, bar one, was horse-drawn, and this mare, Laura by name, was one of the literally hundreds of thousands of horses captured in that country by the British. Thanks to a horse-minded C in C, Major Allhusen was able to buy Laura, and later, in 1947, transport her to Britain, all for the modest outlay of fifty pounds.

Once home, and having already discovered Laura's considerable jumping capabilities in Italy and Austria, Major Allhusen competed with her in show-jumping and hunter trials until tendon trouble retired her to stud. She was sent to Davy Jones – but for a broken rein, a winner of the Grand National – and Laurien was foaled in 1950.

Once broken, by Allhusen methods a gradual, patient process, the little, highly-strung, dark bay mare quickly began to make her mark in the newly emerging sport of eventing. She and Major Allhusen went with the British team that won the European Championships in Copenhagen in 1957, and came fifth as individuals. In '58 she was second at both Badminton and Harewood – the equivalent of Burleigh – they won the Combined Training at the Horse of the Year Show, and, on points, she was British Horse Trial Champion both in that and the following year. Again with a place in the British team for the European Championships – where Britain came second to the Germans by 0.3 of a point – and a third in the individual placings, Laurien ended up the 1958 season as the best event horse in the country, and with a more than good chance of being picked as a member of the Olympic team competing in Rome in 1960. Lameness however put paid to that, and when she went lame again after Badminton in '61, Laurien was also retired to stud. This was when Lochinvar came on the scene.

Bred by Battleburn out of a near Thoroughbred mare by Isolation, Lochinvar, sold as a four-year-old but in reality only three, arrived in England looking like the proverbial 'hat-rack'. In true Irish fashion he had been hunted hard as a two-year-old, and with no opportunity to fill out and muscle up he was a real 'debility case', his looks and condition in no way improved by being covered in warts. Nor were his lack of apparent attractions confined to his physical state. Badly broken and full of bad habits, he had been caught in the back teeth by the ham-handed riders who had jumped him out hunting and was apprehensive about his mouth. With a weak back, a legacy of being ridden when too young that was always to plague him, and with no muscle over the loins, he took the greatest exception to the leg aids and any idea of going forward. Had his owner realised Lochinvar's true age, and had Laurien not gone lame, the young horse, also a bay but 16.3 hands and with a very high wither, would have been given a year off altogether, and as it was, through that winter he was only worked very gently in the school, and on the lunge.

By 1963 Major Allhusen was trying Lochinvar in his first Horse Trials. He was looking a very different animal but, still frightened of his mouth, was not showing a great deal of promise as a jumper, and it was not until '64 that things started to look up. He did quite well at Tidworth towards the end of the year and was placed, and but for a shocking round in the show-jumping, would have won. By the Burghley Horse Trials his owner had torn a muscle and the ride on Lochinvar was given, at a moment's notice, to a girl who was on a non-starter that was also an Allhusen horse. With no opportunity to get to know each other, the result was very encouraging – a second place to a well-known rider at Lochinvar's first top-class Three Day Event.

Obviously this horse had great potential, especially across country, and the British selectors were beginning to sit up and take notice. At one stage there was even some idea of asking the Allhusens' to lend the horse for training on for the next Olympics, but on account of age, no mention was made of including his owner.

They started off well at Badminton in 1965 and were lying fifth after a fast clear round in the cross-country phase but after a disastrous four fences down in the show jumping they fell to eighth place. Despite this, Lochinvar's performance was sufficiently impressive to get him short-listed for the British team all set for Russia and the European Championships that autumn, and after he and his owner had beaten all the other 'possibles' at the final team trials at Eridge, there could be no question of excluding either of them.

No equestrian team had ever been to Russia before, and none was to go again until the European Championships held at Kiev in 1973. The horses were flown out separately and Lochinvar, on his first flight, took a dim view of the entire proceeding. Nowadays horses travel by air in comfort, bedded on peat in wide individual crates, with enclosed fronts but made so that the horses can reach their haynets and the grooms can reach their horses – to provide reassurance if necessary. Entry is *via* a special loading ramp on the same level, then the loaded stalls, in units of three, are raised by scissor-lift to the height of the air-craft and pushed along the hold on rollers, to be securely locked in position. All very easy and different from Lochinvar's reluctant scramble up a ramp, into a narrow and claustrophobic stall, one of those fixed in pairs to the body of the air-craft, with only a partition between the horses.

In fact none of the other horses made any demur, but soon after take-off Lochinvar decided the only way to cope with the situation was to lie down – a potentially fatal move in a partition made specially too narrow for such an event. And he was only dissuaded by the heroic and hazardous work of the vet and the farrier, who managed to get slings under his stomach and then held him virtually in suspension for the entire flight. No-one had any desire to have to repeat such an exercise, and for the return journey Lochinvar travelled in a crate specially flown out from Britain.

A safe arrival at Moscow Airport was not the end to that night's adventures. The riders had arrived shortly before, but a ramp was necessary to unload the horses, and a crane was necessary to unload the ramp from the plane. There was no crane, and when it arrived at 2 am, after a wait of three and a half hours, one of the horses took a quick look at Russia and then declined to unload. Persuasion triumphed in the end, and there remained only the trek out by Army vehicle to the stabling at Moscow racing stadium. But first there was all the forage, heavy tack and mass of equipment to unload from the plane, and it was another two hours before the task of getting the horses aboard could commence.

Not by any stretch of the imagination could those three-ton lorries have been termed suitable horse-transport. There was no canopy, the sides of the vehicles were no higher than three feet, and each was divided into two with a length of tubular rail. Each pair of horses had to scramble aboard up that same steep ramp, onto a metal floor where the only covering was a scatter of hay collected out of the plane. They stood facing forwards, and as dawn broke Major Allhusen and Richard Meade, like the other riders, found themselves seated apprehensively on benches, back to the cab, with their horses' heads in their laps.

The young soldiers who were driving were obviously in need of their breakfasts and intent on wasting no time on the twenty-five miles to Moscow stadium. As they careered on their way the horses slid and slithered trying to keep their feet, low-hanging boughs swept across the tops of their heads . . . and not one of them, not even Lochinvar, so much as batted an eyelid! On arrival they found first-class stabling, equipped even with the luxury of automatic water bowls.

In the competition the British team, handicapped by one horse that could not be hurried over the course, came a commendable third, and Lochinvar was eighth in the Individual. He made no objections to a fast riding steeplechase course that included every kind of weird obstacle – walls set on banks, a 5 foot 6 inch brush with a huge ditch in front – instead of the conventional British birch fences, and went fast and clear.

The cross-country was in the main straightforward and very fair, and the only really questionable obstacle, a Russian speciality, of a fence off a bank and over a rail into deep water, had been vetoed by the Course Inspector. Lochinvar took no exception to jumping a wooden bank painted, as might be expected, in red, and found nothing odd about a fence in the middle of a river composed of an upturned boat, pegged down to keep it in position. Again he was very fast and clear, his score across country the second best in the championship, and it was these two phases that had pulled him up from fortieth, very nearly bottom, where he was placed after the dressage. With a better test in that Phase One, he must have finished amongst the first three horses.

Dressage was always to be Lochinvar's bugbear, and in retrospect Major Allhusen thinks perhaps he should have been tougher with the horse over his aversion to this form of exercise, and also, in the early days, stricter with him about show-jumping. But there were mitigating circumstances of which his rider was only too aware.

When Lochinvar, during a dressage test, swished his tail, or ground his teeth, put his ears back or looked, as one Swedish judge was to remark; 'As though he had thistle spines under his saddle!' he was, as they rightly adjudged, showing every sign of being intensely resentful 'to the leg'. He resented any weight on his back, but the cause of his ire probably lay in the subconscious memory of those painful months in Ireland, when as a gangling baby with no back muscles to take the weight, ignorant riders with legs stuck forward and sitting well back on his loins, went bump . . . bump . . . bump on his tender back arch. The damage that can be done to a young horse's back in this way is appalling; a horse, like an elephant, remembers these things and they are never eradicated. Unlike his successor, Laurieston, Lochinvar was not a naturally supple horse anyway, although he was much helped by a course of electrical treatment given by an osteopath.

Once he had learned to gallop across country, Lochinvar was always to be in his element. His owner hunted him in Leicestershire several times and in such circumstances he proved a terrific hunter, and loved it as much as he was to love getting to grips with any kind, or height of obstacle, as he sped round the cross country phase of a Three Day Event. And although once in the Dressage ring he was always to recall the discomfort in his back, and his behaviour occasionally could appear 'bolshie' to some judges, Lochinvar's overall brilliance turned him into a worthy champion in the annals of Eventing.

In 1966 he broke a blood vessel. To the selection committee this seemed the end of a good horse, but his owner was convinced it was caused entirely through feeding too much protein, a diagnosis, confirmed by the vet, that proved correct. Lochinvar was to recover fully, but in the meantime he missed being included in the British World Championship Team, and was not even being considered for the coming Olympics in Mexico, where the altitude was much in mind.

At Badminton the next year a disastrous round in the final, the show-jumping phase, pulled Lochinvar down from second place to eleventh, but despite this he was picked for inclusion in the British team competing in the European Championships in Ireland. He was again bottom but one in the Dressage, but his brilliance in the steeplechase and cross-country phases and a clear round show jumping pulled him up into third place, and the British Team won — for the first time since his owner and Laurien had represented their country at Copenhagen ten years before.

1968 saw Lochinvar, pulled down by his show-jumping, placed

only fifth at Badminton, but in the team and all set for Mexico and the Olympics.

It was a marvellous flight in an Air France Boeing 707, with highly efficient organisation, level platform, beautiful boxes and a fork-lift. The riders, already in the country as advance party, met their horses off the plane around midnight, and were promptly required, by the totally unexpected Mexican Ministry of Agriculture regulations, to stringently disinfect each animal – a measure against the Foot and Mouth that Britain was supposed to harbour as an endemic disease.

The show-jumpers were included in the party, and this entailed high pressure hosing each horse with a very strong disinfectant, and each had then to be dried. The girl grooms were in bed and in possession of the padlock keys to the saddlery boxes, so these had to be broken open to find the most necessary sweat-scrapers. When they could not then be located the only substitutes were the riders' handkerchiefs, which proved inadequate towels in ratio to the expanse of horse.

Four days of quarantine followed by a further six for acclimatisation, meant a long time off work, and a possible but unwanted gain in weight, for horses required to compete a fortnight later fit for the most gruelling of tests. The altitude of Mexico City and then of Avandaro, only a 1,000 feet lower, where they moved after four days, presented many problems, but their vet's previous and brilliant investigations kept all the horses up to scratch. Digestive troubles were defeated by stringent rationing until work re-started, with bedding on wood shavings instead of edible straw, and high fibre content nuts to eat instead of oats. The water organisms that can have a desperate effect on horses and humans alike, were defeated, in the animals' case, by drinking only filtered water.

Because of the imponderable effects of altitude the cross-country course appeared unexpectedly small, but the heat and heavy going in the first part of the competition, and the rain – the torrential, indescribable torrents of rain that should have ceased by that date but came in the second half, altered the whole picture.

Lochinvar, going as Number One, avoided the blinding sheets of water that made the fences almost unseeable and turned the river to a flood, but had to contend with difficulties over the river crossings, six in all, where the landings were very soft, and despite the applied gravel and sand the horses broke through the surface – a great many to stick and turn over.

Until Lochinvar, always careful with this type of fence and taking off beautifully, seemed to come to a sudden halt on landing that nearly shot his rider off, Major Allhusen did not realise that the horse's feet were breaking through the crust, and in fact he pulled off both front shoes during his round. But apart from that, and one stop, only his second in nineteen Three Day Events, the big bay horse gave a marvellous, secure ride, jumping safely over the water fences where horse after horse came to grief.

With a good Dressage score and a lovely clear round in the show-jumping, Lochinvar had the honour of being second overall, a worthy member of the contingent that won that Gold Medal for Great Britain. He thus won the Silver Medal in the Individual, and but for that one most uncharacteristic stop, he would have made it a double Gold.

Sadly, because of a cold, caught in the good cause of money-raising for a hunt, Lochinvar did not get to Badminton in 1969, a year where, because of his improved show-jumping, his chances of a win were even higher than usual. But he did go to Normandy to help the British team again win the European Championships. And at the end of that year, over-fresh from an enforced rest while his rider re-covered from an injury, he distinguished himself by bucking Major Allhusen off during the parade at the Horse of the Year Show, right in front of the Royal Box and directly under the eyes of Princess Anne.

Not long before this somewhat undignified exhibition, Lochinvar had appeared to be 'feeling' his feet, particularly on hard ground, but as Major Allhusen was laid up with a broken leg all through 1970, the horse was rested anyway.

They got going again together the next year, but although Lochinvar still tackled his fences bravely, he was not so happy jump-ing when a big drop was involved. Then he stopped twice, which was totally out of character, in a couple of Hunter Trials, and later got eliminated at Badminton – for the only time in his life except for his very first attempt at an Event.

There would be no more. Lochinvar had jumped over 800 fences without giving his rider a fall; he had only two stops in the cross-country phase of nineteen successive Three Day Events, and he had helped win a Gold Medal and two European Championships for the British team as well as a Silver Medal for himself. Major Allhusen had always vowed he would retire his horse the moment he showed real disinclination to jump and that was the moment.

Now Lochinvar shares a field with Laurien, while Laurieston, the mare's famous son, continues the story. He is a young horse, already famous throughout the world for winning a double Gold at the Munich Olympics, and his life is still before him. He is a fine successor to the doughty old warrior who overcame the ignorant and damaging handling of his youth to become Lochinvar, the champion of so many years of Eventing.

15
LUCKY STRIKE

It's a long, tiring haul by road from the heat and dust of Spain, across the Channel and so to Ardingly in Sussex, the site of the South of England Show. In 1972 the horse-boxes carrying show-jumpers belonging to the Masarellas made the trek, and travelling only by day arrived at 9 pm on the Wednesday, the next to last day of the show. It was cold, the raw cold of one of the worst of English summers, and made more noticeable after the soaring temperatures of Madrid.

Most of the horses were affected by the rapid change of climate and one of the younger animals took weeks to get over it, but it made no difference to Lucky Strike. As a sixteen-year-old he always found travelling a rest, and it would take more than a drop in the thermo-meter to dull his natural exuberance. The next day he bounded into the arena, in high spirits and fortunately in a mood to concentrate, and jumped his way round the last class to take the South of England Show Jumping Championship.

It was a notable victory in itself but there was more to it than that. Ten years before, at the old Richmond Royal Show that is now incor-porated in the big event at Ardingly, Lucky Strike had also had a big win. But that time there were no painted show jumps to gladden his heart and light his eye, and set him shaking his head and coming on and off the bit in his eagerness to get at them. Ten years before he was moving round the ring so lightly he seemed to be dancing, with 'pointed toe' and long, relaxed stride demonstrating the brilliance of his paces, with neck flexed and correctly bent at the poll and jaw relaxed, and ready at the lightest aid from his rider to put on a 'show' for the judges that would be the epitome of mannered elegance. On that far-off day at Richmond, Lucky Strike won another championship – for the best Large Hack in the show.

This handsome, 15.3-hand, dark brown horse came originally from Cornwall. One or two of his relations made names for themselves as point to pointers; he was sired by the premium stallion, The Admiral, his dam was three-quarter bred and his grand-dam a Dartmoor pony. As a three-year-old he was bought by Count Robert Orssich for the late Mr Hugh Haldin, the owner of those famous show animals including Earmark, Free As Air and Marksman.

Count Orssich knows more about producing hacks for the show ring than any man alive, and possibly if Lucky Strike had fallen into the hands of anyone other than the 'master' his story might have been a very different one. For despite his wonderful movement and all the fire and beauty that adds up to the 'presence' of this great horse, he was not an easy animal to school, and to describe him as being a 'bit of a boy' is the understatement of the day. On the other hand if anyone had had so little understanding of such a character as to designate him a rogue, they would also in truth have had to admit he was an honest one. In his early days as a hack Lucky Strike never tried to 'cover up', he either behaved or he did not, and since changing his role to that of show-jumper he has either jumped brilliantly or spoiled his chances through carelessness, but would never dream of stopping.

Lucky Strike was produced as a four-year-old in the early '60s. His trainer's infinite patience and tact were complemented in the ring by the skill of Anne Davey, Count Orssich's pupil who always rode for him. And gradually the horse came to accept his role – but not without some lively displays more suited to rodeo than a hack class, and certainly not required of an animal expected to display itself as a beautiful, obedient riding horse. Several judges found themselves treated to a ride considerably more exciting than desirable, and on his debut at the Royal Windsor Show, Lucky Strike enlivened the refined atmosphere of a hack class held beneath the ancient walls of the Castle, with some out of place squeals and joyous bucks, plus a marked tendency to cart Anne Davey out of the ring!

But Lucky Strike did settle eventually, or as much as could be expected of such an exuberant character, and then there were few to touch him. He won at shows all over the country, and in his most successful years, 1961, '62, and '63, his numerous victories, in addition to that championship at Richmond in '62, included Reserve Champion at Windsor that same year, as well as best Large Hack at the Royal International and Horse of the Year Shows where he was also Reserve Champion to his stable-mate, Free As Air. He vindicated his initial gaffe at Windsor by taking the championship there in 1963.

Lucky Strike's very successful career as a show hack came to an end when Mr Haldin decided to give up, and both this horse and the show hunter Marksman were presented to Anne Davey. She was by then Mrs Ross, living in Ireland, and when she took both horses there Lucky Strike's function changed from hack to hunter. For the next two seasons he carried his new owner to hounds, and though banks and stone walls came alike to him, no doubt at times he gave her an even more exciting ride than those of his early days in the show ring.

When Mrs Ross decided she could not keep both horses, Marksman remained in Ireland and Lucky Strike returned to England where, with Hugh Haldin's approval he was sold to a showing acquaintance, but on condition that he was not shown again.

Christine Harries had known her new purchase in the show-ring, but otherwise her only knowledge of him before buying was when he was brought into her yard and she sat on his back long enough to pop over a couple of little practice fences. Up to then although she could jump, her activities in public had been confined to showing. But she had always wanted a show-jumper and the feel this horse gave her, the way he was 'rarin' to get over obstacles of a kind never encountered before, thrilled her that day and continued to do so each time she jumped him. So with a rider as inexperienced as himself, Lucky Strike then proceeded on a round of Foxhunter and Grade C classes, mostly with marked success. There were also two ventures into the equally unfamiliar scene of Eventing, and they were placed at Liphook. But although he possessed the marked ability and speed to go across country brilliantly, for all his hack's training it was very plain that dressage was not Lucky Strike's *forte*.

Christine Harries and Lucky Strike stayed together for two years, and in the end it was the horse's obvious and brilliant potential that parted them. His rider was an amateur at the game, with the lower grades her limit. She knew she could not do such an animal justice and when they did make a mistake she always felt the fault was more her's than his. Much as she would have loved to keep Lucky Strike, she knew he warranted a rider to match his implicit greatness, and once again the luck embodied in the horse's name came to the fore.

Alan Oliver had jumped him once or twice in bigger shows and was to do so again at Aldershot in 1967. On the day he had no time and Christine asked her friend Malcolm Pyrah, the well-known show-jumper who rode for the Masarella stable and happened to be there, if he would do so instead. So Malcolm climbed on to the back of a horse he had never seen before and won the class under the knowledgeable eyes of John Masarella, watching from the ringside and sufficiently impressed to buy Lucky Strike there and then.

And again the luck held, because Malcolm Pyrah is one of the few riders with the infinite patience and understanding to bother with 'making a good job' of such a talented but erratic performer, a horse whose exuberance is his greatness . . . but can equally be his downfall.

Nor was it a question of bringing on a youngster slowly to the game, an animal with many years of jumping up on the peak before him. Lucky Strike was then eleven years old, yet by show-jumping standards scarcely out of novice grade. He had to get to the top quickly before sheer age inevitably set him on the downward slope, and despite a few remaining difficulties, this is exactly what he did.

Malcolm found his new horse friendly and quiet in the stable, a calm, unfussed traveller and a good trencherman – provided he never sees anything being put into his food. The least suspicion of the most innocuous tonic being added to a feed, and Lucky Strike will not even approach his meal. He does not winter out, but used to be put out for the odd hour and quite often in the summer, a proceeding that always enlivened the scene for the other horses. For Lucky

Strike would at once pick up any sizeable stick, a stake even, and go careering round the field with it in his teeth, either of intent or by accident whacking his companions as he went. He has always been exercised in the paddocks, and since he uses anything from a shadow to an approaching lorry as the perfect excuse for taking off over the nearest hedge, no-one expresses any great desire to ride him on the road.

With his innate drop of pony cleverness Lucky Strike had little difficulty in adapting to the requirements of a top-class show-jumper. He quickly disproved the theory that the straight leg action of the show hack makes it difficult to bend the knee sufficiently to jump big fences. His length of stride has never given problems at the combination fences that he jumps so well, and he has always had sufficient respect for water to clear it by yards. The only legacy of his hack training that does make Lucky Strike an awkward horse to jump, is that he carries his head like a show-horse, and unless he literally cannot help himself will never use his neck. Instead of rounding his back and stretching neck and head in the way most helpful to making height and spread, he tends to hold his neck back in the collected position he was taught when young.

When it comes to temperament, maturity had at least sobered this horse beyond the degree of youthful 'gassiness' that could have persuaded even Malcolm Pyrah that he would not make a worthwhile show-jumper, but how he goes in any competition still rests almost entirely with Lucky Strike. He has proved he has the scope for any course, however big, but whether he will fool around and through carelessness or inattention have a couple of fences down, depends entirely on how he is feeling. And that is something that he nearly always makes plain to his rider, during exercise and long before they go into the ring.

With this horse it's a question of travelling him and just waiting hopefully for the right day. He has gone to the Royal International and had the first fence down in the King's Cup one day, and come out the next evening to win his class hands down. When he chooses to perform he is fantastic, when he does not it's no use worrying about it – it will not make any difference! Half his trouble is that he is a born show-off, he will start playing to the gallery instead of paying attention to the job in hand, but however big the fences and however much he is playing around, Lucky Strike is far too clever to get into any trouble. Maybe he would concentrate if he did, but everything he does you have to accept, because he is that kind of a horse.

In his novice days Lucky Strike always played second fiddle to his famous stable-mate, Mr Softee, but soon he was to prove himself a champion in his own right and emerged out of the background. Horses often go better at a particular time of the year, and this one always goes very well at the beginning of the season. He needs none of the more usual jumping at a show or two to get confident again after the winter rest, and will go straight into an International class and deal with the big fences as though he had been jumping for weeks. And at a show he needs no warming up at all, anything more than once over a practice pole will send him mad with excitement. The older he gets the better he goes at shows indoors. Originally the atmosphere, magnified by an enclosed space, was altogether too much for him, but age, combined with a couple of cotton-wool ear-plugs that allow him to hear what his rider has to say but tone down the electrifying atmosphere, have worked wonders.

On his trips abroad, on his day, Lucky Strike makes nothing of the natural obstacles he may encounter, but although those at Hickstead are very similar he dislikes that course, maybe because most horses come first to the novice classes there but he had to wade straight in at Grade A. He has come down the notorious bank used in the Jumping Derby twice in safety, and in the Derby of 1972 was one of the two horses only that jumped the 'bogey' fence, the Devil's Dyke, without penalty, yet he has never got round Hickstead without making a nonsense of one or another of the comparatively simple obstacles.

Inconsistency is Lucky Strike's downfall. If not on the actual short list, he was very much in mind when it came to choosing the British Team for the 1972 Olympics, and he came second in two of the guinea-pig trials, one at the Royal Highland and the other at the Yorkshire. But then he tipped on his head over the easiest fence at Hickstead in the third trial, and that was that. And maybe it was as well because in the Olympics you cannot have a horse with all the ability in the world, that can yet say: 'I don't want to know . . . today . . .'

Wherever he goes in the south, the fans of his showing days are there to cheer Lucky Strike on. There was a good sprinkling of them at Wembley at the Horse of the Year Show in 1971, but the fences were small that year and Lucky Strike, a cocky horse, was treating them with more complacency than Malcolm Pyrah thought good for his soul. He decided therefore to take him in for a couple of rounds in the Puissance just to give him something to think about, and then retire. It seemed a good idea even though the highest his horse had ever jumped was 5 foot 10 inches – and that is a hefty fence. It was a decision that did give the show hack fans something to cheer about, in common with everyone else. For Lucky Strike came prancing in, arrestingly handsome, covering the ground with his great stride, shaking his head and coming on and off the bit and generally show-ing off as usual, until he faced those fences and decided they were worthy of his attention. Then there was no more playing about. Each time they went up he cleared them, until in the end he sailed effort-lessly over that huge, menacing wall that was built up to 7 foot, and won the first puissance competition of his life.

Since then, and to prove it was not a flash in the pan, there has been another puissance, the Test in Madrid. Again Lucky Strike cleared 7 foot, even more easily this time, but he did not win because he had the spread down to come third.

It is obvious this horse can jump any height, any day he wants to. If in the mood he is equally at home on tough courses in Spain, or winning competitions like the Matthew Brown-sponsored 'Champion of Champions' he took at the Royal Lancashire in 1970, or the Ever-est Double Glazing, one of the largest courses and most important events of the Royal International, that he won in 1972. He is a great horse, and a great character, and has the unique distinction of having hit the peak in the two spheres of equine competing that lie furthest apart. Only Lucky Stike can lay claim to being both a cham-pion Show Hack and a champion Show Jumper.

16

STROLLER

The path to Stroller's field leads through a copse where oak trees tower overhead, and a thicket of brambles provides cover for the odd rabbit or two, the delight of the Mould's Jack Russell terrier. The paddock is large, with hedges for windbreaks and trees for shade, and there, as he was on a glorious day in December 1972, is Stroller himself – comfortably shaggy, showing obvious traces of the last enjoyably muddy roll, and lording it over the two or three horses and ponies that keep him company in his retirement.

Within minutes of meeting Stroller in the flesh two popular misconceptions are rectified. For all the lovely long front and powerful quarters this is not just a miniature horse. Maybe the Irish pony that was his mother did jump into a field where she had no business to be, and so provided her son with a proportion of Thoroughbred blood through his sire, but Stroller is essentially a genuine, charming pony – a bay with black points, a white star on his face and a white sock on his near hind leg. When he moves, however, he does display the lengthy stride of a horse. When he trots, head up and surveying the scene with the justified air of a conqueror, it is easy to go along with those who – after watching Stroller in the ring 'growing' the inches that he seemed to put on for the occasion, and surrounded by the aura that proclaimed 'Here's a champion!' – used to approach his rider and say: 'You can't tell *me* he's only 14.2 hands!' But get close up beside his shoulder and you realise, like those who visited him in his stable after a competition, that it is the indefinable something called 'presence' that gives Stroller his illusion of size. In fact he is no more than the $14.1\frac{1}{2}$ hands claimed as his official height.

In his heyday Stroller always seemed to know that he was 'a bit special', a concept that has not lessened since he stopped jumping to enjoy a happy, very well-earned old age. And now even if there were the remotest likelihood of Marion Mould lessening the good care she gives the pony who filled her life for so many years, Stroller himself would see to it that he was not neglected. In the months when he was turned out at grass, resting after each strenuous jumping season, the pony was always brought in at night to a thick bed in a warm stable, and that is still his by right. Nowadays, if the weather is too wet or too cold for his liking, Stroller refuses to venture out at all, and on the very occasional evenings when the Moulds return what he considers to be a little late, he jumps the gate from the paddock and puts himself to bed.

Marion Coakes, as she was then, first saw Stroller at a small local show, when she was thirteen. There was something about his make-up, the way he moved, the way he popped over the low fences, that caught her eye, and she told her father. At the time the Coakes' were looking for another pony for their daughter, and when Mr Coakes caught up again with this particular one, a few weeks later at the Horse of the Year Show, he outbid several other would-be buyers and brought Stroller back to their farm in Hampshire.

The pony was then about seven years old, and although he had been pottering around gymkhanas for a while and had collected three or four first prizes in the process, he was still a comparative novice. A status that remained until the following jumping season, after a winter spent in just riding around getting mutually acquainted.

The only difficulty appeared to be with Stroller's mouth, a trouble, common with Irish horses and ponies that is due largely to hasty and unskilled breaking, and was to remain all through his jumping career.

Stroller is a strong pony and proved a real tearaway to school at home, a foible hard to believe by those who came to know the calm, business-like Stroller of the show-ring, where he was even liable to drop his bit and need riding well up into his bridle at the start of a competition.

In fact the pony has such a lot of natural ability that he needed very little schooling at all, and since working him at home was never easy, most of Stroller's training consisted of road work to get him fit. Not that he was the quietest of hacks, for although impervious to traffic, he is the type to find it amusing to shy at the same piece of paper in the hedge for five days running, and then to have hysterics because it is missing on the sixth! But if schooling over fences in the home paddock was not a large part of the training programme, and hunting was 'out' because it excited him to the verge of lunacy, that did not preclude jumping. From the age of nine when she used to exercise her brother's 'Grade A' jumpers, Marion Coakes had been in the habit of taking off over anything, of any height or width, that took her fancy. And much of the complete mutual confidence that pony and rider quickly established, stems from those hours out on exercise when the way always either led straight ahead regardless – or included any intriguing diversions to either hand such as a five-bar gate, padlocked against intruders, or the steep-banked ditch dividing a neighbour's field.

Their first show together was at Brockenhurst, five miles from home. It turned out to be a memorable affair, but not only because Stroller jumped clear. That was entirely as expected, the imponderable was the fence, a double, that Marion, – thrilled with her super pony, confident of defeating the opposition in a virtual walk-over – missed out in the general excitement . . . and they were eliminated for taking the wrong course!

After that salutary lesson in concentration and the perils of over-confidence, the Marion Coakes-Stroller combination quickly soared to the top in Junior competing, and remained there for the next two years. It is some measure of Stroller's quality and success that in 1962, working four or five days a week, he concluded seven weeks of competetive jumping without having a single fence down. An achievement highlighted by winning £600 that season, in the years when the first prize in Junior jumping classes was usually no more than £3 or £4, with perhaps £10 at a really big show.

The biggest thrill came at the end of 1962, when Marion and Stroller were included in the Junior European team, victorious that year in Berlin. In those days the team was always picked from 16–18 year old 'Young Riders', so that it was a real measure of their meteoric success that a fifteen year old and a pony, should be picked to represent their country and jump against 'Open' horses.

Marion officially left the Junior jumping scene behind when she was sixteen, and the last few months before she started in Open classes were punctuated with family argument. Good as Stroller was, her family felt it would be unrealistic to expect a pony to jump against horses – over the formidable courses that must come his way if his rider was to achieve her ambitions. But she was adamant. Stroller was something special, and she was sure his long stride would be better suited by the distances between Open combinations. After the success with the Junior European team in Berlin, she and Stroller had gone on with them to Copenhagen, where they tackled their first really big show, a Concours Hippique International Officiel. And despite the pony's size the fences had not appeared frighteningly big, and the occasion had confirmed Marion's never-to-waver faith in Stroller's ability to jump, at speed, anything he might encounter.

Mr Coakes was not the only one to question his daughter's wisdom in 'taking a pony into horses', and despite her reiterated opinion that of course she could . . . because Stroller *was* something special, it reached the point where, at the Blackpool Show, Ann Moore actually tried out Stroller with a view to buying him. But although she got on well with the pony the price was outside the Moores' range, and to Marion's relief Stroller returned home with her to Hampshire.

In 1962 they began their first season in Open Jumping, doing the usual round of shows known as 'the circuit'. Three years later, by the combined effort of Stroller's brilliance and her own exceptional ability, Marion Coakes became Ladies World Champion – at the tender age of eighteen – a title only to be gained by the genuinely versatile rider and horse, capable of dealing with three or four different types of competition and where the emphasis is on speed. She was also the youngest ever holder of the Queen Elizabeth II Cup, a member of Britain's three times successful Nations Cup team, and voted the

Daily Express and Sports' Writers' Sportswoman of the Year.

Normally one would pick a prospective top-class show-jumper with the quality and size to provide the scope necessary for big fences, but every rule has its exception and Stroller is the exception with a capital 'E'. He has of course the powerful back and strong, muscular second-thighs that are other essentials to success in this field, and with them the outstanding courage and spring that put him in a class by himself. As his rider had foreseen, the pony's length of stride was better suited to the distances between the fences in Open Jumping, and the same complete confidence in his rider that she had in him, turned every course, however big, into a happy challenge. All types of fence, upright, spread, combination, seemed to come alike to Stroller, even water, so often a bugbear to the best, presented no problems, and he took it so high, with so splendid a bascule, that he could clear 18 feet without undue effort.

Although aloof with strangers, Stroller has always been sweet natured and easy to handle in the stable, and wherever he is, however strange the surroundings, he eats well – so long as he gets his food in small appetising quantities, and not in an off-putting heap. His calm acceptance of any form of travel from horse box to plane, and for any length of time, was a big asset in these days of travelling great distances between shows.

Through the years Stroller rapidly became a legend. Like any horse or pony the world over he had the occasional 'off' day, but he had the heart not of one but of several lions, a bouncy leap and handiness that never seemed to fail, and the speed that is usually the deciding factor in big competitions. Above all his very apparent enjoyment of the sport remained undiminished.

He obviously loved the wide open spaces of Hickstead, making a speciality of that famous course where he was to win the record of five 'Golds', a gold medal being the annual award for amassing the most points at the course in one season. The first time he and his rider encountered the unique, notorious and in their day still unmodified 10 foot 6 inch bank, Marion regarded it as an acceptable challenge – an understandable view-point since they went clear over the course that day. But although Stroller coped with this obstacle five or six times in his career and each time arrived at the bottom without mishap, he only once came down it correctly. The other occasions involved a bit of a scramble, achieved by his innate pony cleverness in somehow 'finding a spare leg'. His rider also felt that, as with herself, Stroller liked the bank less each time he met it.

The 1967 season was concluded in a blaze of glory, winning the Jumping Derby, and the second of those gold medals at Hickstead for the second year running, and then shattering the formidable opposition in the important Philip's Electrical Stakes at the Horse of the Year Show, with a faultless 38.2 seconds round in the timed barrage. They had been part of the victorious British team for the Nations Cup in Rotterdam, and had won two events in America. Then it was 1968 and the year of the Olympics in Mexico.

Here was the peak opportunity, the acme of ambition for the world's top athletes and horsemen, with weeks of growing tension before each nation's teams were picked. Judged only on his record it seemed impossible to leave Stroller out of Britain's show jumping team, but there was still the vital question. Could a pony, however phenomenal, possibly jump the enormous fences and fierce combinations of an Olympic course designed for big, strong horses?

Stroller left the selectors little option. At the principal shows between April and August that year he won: two 1sts and a 3rd at the Hickstead Spring Jumping Tournament; a 1st and two 2nds at the Devon County; a 1st at the Surrey County, and another at the South of England Show; a championship at Butlins – which made the third win in a row – yet another championship, and an Area International Trial. He netted a 1st and the Championship at the Royal Show and the Wills International at Hickstead. Victory in the Jumping Derby there clinched the matter beyond all doubt, and the successes abroad – a 2nd in the Premio Esquilimo, a tied 3rd in the finals of the Women's European Championships, and the Victor Ludorum taken at the Premio Generale Fulgosi at Rome – merely strengthened his rider's unshaken faith in her pony's ability to jump any fence they came to.

The team left for Mexico on 23 September to give the horses the required time to become acclimatised before the first competition, the Individual Grand Prix, to take place just under a month later. Stroller, showing his usual aplomb about travelling, took the long flight in his stride, and settled at once into strange surroundings where the atmosphere might be rarified, but where horses and riders alike could enjoy the good organisation and accomodation provided by their Mexican hosts.

The time slipped by very fast, with no troubles and everything going according to plan until about a week before the Individual competition, when suddenly Stroller started shaking his head. He appeared dull of eye and uncharacteristically listless, and when a foul discharge poured from one nostril it was obvious something was very wrong. The British vet, Mr Scott-Dunn, quickly discovered the cause, a rotten back tooth, split down the centre that had become septic and was affecting the sinus on that side. The tooth would have to come out, but both the timing and the place were wrong, and the vet felt that so long as Stroller responded quickly to the temporary treatment of pain-killers and inhalations of steam, the extraction could safely be delayed. Whether he would be fit enough to compete remained in the balance, while for three days he could not be ridden at all, and showed his discomfort by walking around his box with the ear on the bad side flat against his head. Then with equal suddeness the pony started to perk up, he could be worked and was performing well over practice fences. And on the day that was to be the culmination of his brilliant career Stroller was showing no appreciable effect of his trouble, apart from his right ear that he still carried slightly back, and an insensitivity on the right-hand side of his mouth that just might prove a problem to his rider.

As Marion, first to go of the British team, waited to enter the ring, she was thankful to find Stroller as cool and calm as usual, and behaving as though an Olympic contest, taking place thousands of feet up in the Mexican mountains, was a frequent occurance in his life.

The pony bounded into that ring at Campo Marte with his usual ebullience, and as the starting bell clanged, his head was up as normal and he was pulling to get at the first obstacle. This first leg of the competition was a formidable course, 750 metres long, with fourteen Nations Cup fences to be jumped in a time limit of 112 seconds — a test that was effectively to sort out the forty-two competitors. Up to the moment of Stroller's round there had been no clears, and it seemed impossible that this diminutive animal could achieve what all the best jumping horses of the world, aided by their superior height and strength, were failing to do. At the enormous parallel bars the pony had to show even greater courage and agility than normal, by launching himself when he was too small even to be able to see the far pole from his take-off, and at some of the other fences he appeared to go almost vertically. But he was jumping superbly, and gave his rider not the slightest qualm until the second to last obstacle, when her fears about his mouth were justified. Unresponsive to the right rein, Stroller came round so wide that they nearly missed out the fence altogether. At the last moment she managed to turn him, but so sharply that he lost impulsion and they were dangerously close to the huge spread. Only exceptional bravery and skill got the pony over that one, with nothing worse than an unpenalising rap to the top bar – then it was four strides to the last fence, and a cracking gallop over the finishing line with roar upon roar of cheering to lend wings to Stroller's heels.

They had achieved an unbelievable clear round, in the type of competition where such a feat is almost unknown, and as the best of the Italian and American horses came in to collect often double figure faults, it seemed as though it might be the only one. But five from last came the great American pair, Bill Steinkraus and his horse Snowbound, and their faultless round, to make the second of the day, clearly pointed to where the main opposition lay.

Sixteen horses, including all four British animals, went through to the second round. The course was reduced to six fences of *puissance* type, including a wall at 5 foot 9 inches, a spread of more than 7 foot at the 5 foot 5 inches triple, and another 7 foot 3 inches spread to that most difficult of jumps, a true parallel now standing at 5 foot 7 inches.

Again Stroller bounded into the ring with his normal verve, and although dwarfed by such a course, made no bones about tackling it with his usual confidence. This time though, a misjudged turn at the huge parallel, followed by too much speed going into the double, produced a total of eight faults. Despite this, Stroller, who had proved over a most formidable course that Olympic fences were within his scope, held his lead in the contest for the Gold Medal – until Bill

Steinkraus and Snowbound clipped one fence, to win with a total of only four faults.

But if Britain was robbed of the individual Gold, the Silver Medal was magnificently captured – to make Marion Coakes the first lady competitor to win an Olympic individual jumping medal, and Stroller the first pony, and probably the last, ever to compete, let alone take second place, in an Olympic competition.

The team event took place four days later in the big Olympic stadium. And while horses are not machines and nothing is certain in this life, it seemed reasonable that the British team should be optimistic of their chances. In the previous competition David Broome riding Mr Softee, had supplemented Stroller's victory by taking third place, and the Bronze Medal, with a brilliant round, and Bill Steinkraus would not be representing the USA in the team event because Snowbound was lame. Obviously this course for the Grand Prix des Nations would be larger and more difficult than any encountered outside an Olympics, but technically judged on measurement alone, it was slightly smaller than that for the Individual.

Stroller's sinus was still discharging down one nostril, but he appeared in good form and was jumping well, with only one niggle of doubt occuring on the last day when he took a few of the practice fences unusually high.

It was a cloudless morning, with the arena gay with brilliantly painted fences, artificial flowers decorating the wings, and a huge colourful crowd filling every available seat. The British team arrived with their confidence still high, where it remained after walking the course and taking due note of the severe combinations and difficult distances between the fences. The imponderable that day was partly in the going, unexpectedly both slippery and holding, that worsened as the hours passed.

Stroller was to go eighth, and it was somewhat unnerving when the seven previous horses, each normally a star performer, all defaulted on time, and none completed a round with a score of less than twenty faults. Yet Stroller made the obstacles appear easy, until he came to the combination. He cleared the initial element, a wall, but then, for the first time in their long career together, his rider was conscious of the tremendous, and in this case unsuccessful, effort he had to make to reach for the second of the parallel poles. It fell, but they sailed on over the next three fences and the following 16 foot of water. Twenty-eight yards beyond was a double, this time of rustic parallels, and as they came into it Stroller was as usual taking a strong hold. It was normal tactics for his rider to steady him, but owing to the mouth trouble the pony over-checked, lost the essential speed, hit the first pole, landed on the second and, found himself, all propulsion gone, between the two elements of the obstacle. He stopped – it was impossible to go on – and although at the second attempt there was no question of his not clearing both parts of what proved a real 'bogey' fence to many other horses, this was the first time Stroller had ever refused – and undoubtedly he was confused and upset by such a happening.

With time faults added, the final score for the round was twenty-one and three-quarters but even so at the end of the first leg of the competition the British team were in the lead with a total of forty-eight faults, with the Canadians close on their heels with forty-nine and a half.

Stroller, the typical showman, always reacts to a crowd and an occasion with extra zest and those added 'inches' he puts on in the ring, but as they came in for the second round of that Grand Prix des Nations, Marion was horrified to realise this was a Stroller she had never known before. The altitude, the poisoned tooth, the exertions of the morning combined with the frightening first experience of 'things going really wrong', had all taken their toll. The pony felt floppy and unwilling, and although she did her best to gather him up, he jumped the first two fences very badly and had the third one down. After that they continued without incident, if without either inspiration or real confidence, until they came to the redoubtable combination. As with the practice fences of the previous day, Stroller jumped much too high at the first part, the wall, and then, all his impulsion expended, stopped again at the first of the parallels.

Quickly they swung round for another attempt, but it was a brave effort that became a disaster. Stroller fell attempting to take off at the parallel, and a falling pole hit his rider in the face. Semi-concussed and bleeding from the nose, she remounted and in a daze made automatically for the exit, until a warning shout from Harvey

Smith turned her and Stroller to face the fence again. This time, somehow, they made it, but in her confused state Marion had omitted to signal the judges to stop the timing clock until she was ready to recommence, and although she and Stroller continued on round without further incident, the time ran out and they were eliminated.

At the time it was unbelievable, it was a disaster, but it was certainly no disgrace, and under Olympic rules it did not mean the elimination of the entire team. Stroller's score, based on the worst round plus twenty additional faults, added up to over seventy but even with that, another great round by David Broome saw to it that Britain came eighth out of fourteen.

Looked at in retrospect, Stroller should have been omitted from the team event, but only on health grounds. Despite his illness he had done brilliantly in the individual competition, but because of his exceptional courage no-one had quite appreciated just how much the sinus trouble, accentuated by altitude, had taken out of him.

There were those who contended that the pony failed because he had been over-faced at fences beyond his scope, but Stroller failed because of his physical condition. Two years before the Olympics he had proved he could make the height – at a *puissance* in Antwerp, entered on impulse in an attempt to 'get' a somewhat cock-sure Harvey Smith. And when Harvey was knocked out in the second round, Stroller went on to clear 6 foot 10 inches and share first prize with Alwin Schockemöhle, riding a horse of nearly 18 hands. Admittedly a plain *puissance* does not entail the fearsome spreads that make an Olympic course the supremely severe test, but there were only two clear rounds in the entire 1968 Olympics ... and Stroller jumped one of them. And nothing that happend afterwards could belittle the Silver Medal that Stroller won for Britain.

On their return to England the pony's tooth was removed, but he took a long time to recover from the sinus trouble, and it was well into 1969 before he was ready to leave the veterinary stables in Berkshire where he had been under the care of Mr Scott-Dunne. Once he was fully recovered and back in training at the Coakes', Stroller was soon proving that his skill and energy were unimpaired. By the end of May he and Marion, by then married to the well-known steeplechase jockey, David Mould, were in Lucerne, as members of the British team that came second in the Prix des Nations. Stroller won the German Jumping Derby in Hamburg a fortnight later. He was the only horse to go clear in the British team that won the Prince of Wales Cup that year, and amongst many other successes came those in the Ladies' World Championship that gave a 2nd in the Final Placings. The confirmation of his brilliant comeback, came when Stroller won the W.D. and H.O. Wills Grand Prix at Hickstead.

By 1970 Stroller was still a top-notch winner. By 1971 he was winning, too, but he was then eighteen years old, and in the nature of things was not quite capable, physically, of what he could do before. He was fit and well and his legs were still as unblemished as the day he was foaled, but at the end of that season when he won the Country Life and Riding Cup at the Horse of the Year Show, Marion Mould felt that her pony had done enough, and that he should leave the scene on that triumphant note. In old age he could never get any better, his career could only go the other way, and instead of continuing to jump Stroller until, inevitably, he was beaten by younger animals, she let him quietly relax into the retirement that was not officially announced until 1973.

Stroller has been ridden since, but over jumping his rider senses that he agrees with the decision – he gives the feeling that he too reckons he has done enough. And if one takes into account, over and above his phenomenal seasonal victories that went on through so many years, the total of £25,500 in prize money, won in Britain alone; the three clear rounds he achieved at Hickstead, where by 1972 only twelve have been jumped, and the Olympic Silver Medal that made him, on merit, the second best show jumper in the entire world, then Stroller has indeed earned his rest.

17
PSALM

Sunday, 3 September 1972; a huge arena, a pentagonal jewel set amongst artificially created hills and lakes, with the gaily-coloured, flower flanked obstacles it contains patterning the grass. And people – 100,000 people cramming the banked surrounds of this Riem Equestrian Stadium, with their build-up of suspense and excitement and momentary despair, with their projected good wishes and sudden frights and tension-relieving spurts of laughter all generating an atmosphere as apparent if intangible as fog, as electrifying as that of the intimate, indoor Horse of the Year Show at the Empire Pool at Wembley. This is Munich, four years after Mexico, Munich and the individual show-jumping contest of the Twentieth Olympic Games.

The course is testing and Olympic in concept as it should be; it needs accurate jumping and an obedient horse but there is no particular fence likely to become a 'bogey', difficult distances but no trick ones to bring the pile-up of faults seen on similar occasions in the past. 'Good and fair' seems to be the overall verdict, yet a real Olympic challenge for these top-flight show-jumpers of the world.

Here is Piero d'Inzeo, now, to show the way, impressive as always but maybe his horse lacks experience? Anyway, it's twelve faults. Tic Tac, with Alfonso Segovia from Spain, he's only had one down; and now it's that powerful horse Hideaway with Mike Saywell, the first

British pair. He's clear up to and over the water – but a bit of trouble with the parallels and, yes, eight faults in all. Steelmaster, he's for Canada but American-bred, has got a second clear, but for the USA Sloopy has dropped a negligent American hoof in the water – and obviously set a bad example because Robin, with Fritz Ligges of the German contingent, has done the same! Surprise, surprise . . . whatever is Nagir up to with Nelson Pessoa? You don't expect a refusal and twenty-one faults from any horse ridden by Brazil's top man, one of the best Grand Prix riders in the world! But then . . . that's show jumping. Fiorello now, he's giving Raimondo, the other one of Italy's famous d'Inzeo brothers a happy ride, so far – but no, it's not their day, he's got twelve faults, too.

Now, here's Manhattan and the world champion David Broome. David's genius lies in getting the best out of every horse he rides, but Manhattan can be unpredictable. Sometimes a crowd atmosphere inspires him, sometimes it makes him scatty and inattentive, but surely, surely today . . . no! He's hit those rails after the water-ditches, he's left a heel on the water tape, too. That's eight faults, and now it's up to Psalm and Ann Moore. But first there is a good clear round by Ambassador and Graziano Mancinelli for Italy to inspire them.

Psalm should like this course. Obviously it's his toughest yet and Olympic form is often, as Manhattan has just shown, unpredictable, but some of it, those water ditches with the straight poles in front of the first and behind the second, and the spaciousness of it all, should remind him of Hickstead. And Psalm likes Hickstead.

He ought to, he has won there often enough. Amongst other victories was that in 1967, the second 'leg' of Ann's Triple Crown that gave her the Young Rider Championship for her second year running. They were equal third in their very first British Jumping Derby at Hickstead when Ann, by then in the adult world of show-jumping, collected a trophy for the best rider under twenty-one. And they won the Hickstead Derby Trial in both 1970, and in 1971 – the season they also collected the Wills Hickstead Medal as the course specialists of the year. It was winning the Wills Grand Prix there earlier in 1972, in the final pre-Olympic trial, that gave Ann Moore and Psalm their undisputed place in the British team.

Certainly Psalm likes the environment this day in Munich. He comes in doing a showing-off, extended trot, head up, ears pricked, alert and reacting to the heady atmosphere of what is, so far, the biggest occasion of his life. And, presented just right at every fence and, with his deer-like leap giving each one a foot to spare, there was never a doubt about this round – a clear, a lovely British clear.

The second round came in the afternoon, with ten enormous, thought-provoking fences to be jumped by the twenty best horses of the morning. The biggest problem – the straight-up white rails, with a re-adjustment of stride necessary to get up to the first part of the third fence – a formidable double of rustic parallels – without losing the vital propulsion.

Hideaway solved that particular one all right, but only to collect sixteen and a quarter faults elsewhere, while Manhattan, in an 'off' mood, had three fences down as well as time faults. Again Britain's bid for a medal in the Individual lay with Ann Moore and Psalm.

You have only to watch them to realise how much this horse relishes jumping, but he took those white rails so big that his rider lost her stirrups, and with no time to find them again in the short distance before the next fence, came into that big double riding virtually bareback. That is not a possible method of coping with Olympic courses, and with the shift in balance as Ann struggled to remain in the saddle and without the expected aids, Psalm was virtually pilotless. He hesitated, sufficiently to make him hit both parts of the obstacle for eight faults, but without sapping his courage to continue both there, and to go on, jumping brilliantly over the remainder of the course.

Three competitors, one each from America, Italy and Britain, all with eight faults, left to jump the final barrage, a formidable, heightened collection of triple bar, white rails, one set of rustic parallels, and the wall, followed by a turn to come into the triple before a spread as last fence.

Sloopy went first – to have two down; then Ambassador, taken with a time-saving if hazardous zig-zag after the wall, to go clear and fast. If Ann and Psalm were to collect their Gold it meant going even faster, as well as faultless.

Knowing the horse it seemed best to save precious seconds on the first part of the course, to leave time for keeping a smooth cadence as they turned at the wall, but the luck was out. A sizzling cut into those big white rails was just a fraction too sharp and Psalm, seeing the fence a fraction too late for take-off, stopped.

The recovery and second attempt were so speedy that no time faults were clocked up, and there were no hesitations or mistakes over the rest of the course – but there were those three points, the penalty for a stop, between Ambassador's final score and Psalm's, and that added up to Britain conceding the Gold Medal to Italy.

Of course it was disappointing, but the award of the Silver Medal, in the end the only medal our show-jumpers were to win, emphasised the great achievement of a young girl and a courageous horse. And the ovation they received from those tens of thousands of spectators, underlined it.

For the Olympic Grand Prix des Nations, the team event held on the final day, the weather swung from warmth and sunshine to arctic temperatures, and Psalm's luck seemed to swing with it. His splendid jumping gave added proof of his ability to cope with all the huge obstacles, bar one – but the distances between the three elements of the treble were particularly difficult for a horse with Psalm's careful, clean style of jumping, and proved his bugbear. In the first round he hit the first two elements and then ran out at the third, and, the memory of that fresh in mind, in the second barrage soared confidently over the course until he came again to the cause of his previous troubles. This time he stopped twice, but at the third attempt responded bravely and made a tremendous and successful effort to clear it, but at a cost of 17 jumping faults and 3.5 for time. He continued clear to complete his fifth Olympic round, over courses which had proved beyond the scope of some of the most experienced show-jumpers in the world.

There's a saying that a good horse never has a bad name, and Psalm, the well-called son of the premium stallion, Sermon, is one that demonstrates its truth. Ann Moore's father, who has been advising his young daughter and managing her horses since her Pony Club days, bought the bay thoroughbred in Yorkshire, as a four-year-old in the winter of 1965.

Although a strong rider, Ann is small and prefers horses that are around sixteen hands, and since she also prefers horses of high courage, more likely to need restraining than urging on, a Thoroughbred is usually her choice.

Psalm measured up to these requirements, and added the intelligence and forceful personality that are his own particularly strong characteristics. He knew nothing of show-jumping or the show-ring, but before coming to the Moore's home in Warwickshire he had been hunted a few times with the Meynell. Exciting, blood-stirring excursions which taught him a lot, but during which he had also discovered the art of occasionally slamming on the brakes and refusing a fence if he felt like it.

Ann always schools her own horses, and during that first winter put in a lot of good work training her new acquisition. Lunging on circles or over cavalletti, jumping only low fences until approach and take-off, obedience and mutual confidence were as they should be, did much to eradicate the habit, but in the earlier days of competing he was still capable, just now and again, of ducking his head and stopping if he reckoned he could get away with it. But Ann soon came to know this horse so well that it was seldom she could not circumvent his efforts, and he became one of the most consistent of show-jumpers. Even so, during the Wills Embassy Stakes in 1971, Psalm either 'came wrong' at a big obstacle or decided, at the last moment it was not to his taste, and caught his rider by surprise with a lightning 'duck out' that gave her a nasty fall.

In 1966, when Psalm first appeared in public, his rider was still only sixteen. It was a good indication of his progress, and of Ann's ability, that they qualified that season for the Foxhunter Trophy at Wembley, and finished runners-up to that distinguished adult pair, David Broome and Top of the Morning. This was heady stuff, and with Psalm really settling down, they went on to Woodstock, to beat Anneli Drummond-Hay and her brilliant horse Merely-a-Monarch, and later chalked up that win at Hickstead in the Wills Young Rider Championship of Great Britain. By the next season Psalm was jumping in Open competitions, and went along as reserve horse when Ann went to Jessolo, near Venice, as a member of the British team that carried off the Junior European Championship.

By 1968 Psalm was Ann's first string for the Young Riders'

Championship, and his fast, calm and collected rounds gave her the title for the second year running, and demonstrated her horse's unmistakable promise for the years to come in adult events. They competed for the coveted Queen Elizabeth Cup at the Royal International Show, but Psalm hit about the easiest fence on the course to put them equal fifth in that competition. However he more than redeemed himself at the Midlands International Show, where his performance in the Junior European Championships gave his rider the Individual medal, and ensured Britain winning the team championship.

Since those early glories Psalm has become well acquainted with life on The Circuit, the show-jumper's world where, during the season much of the horses' lives are spent on the road in their comfortable horse-boxes, and their riders' homes are contained within the four small walls of a caravan. And since 1969 Psalm's circuit has extended to all the major shows in Europe. He has won in La Baule and Copenhagen, at Ostend and Rotterdam, in Germany and over the tough courses found in Madrid. There have been defeats and disappointments – liver trouble, a 'pricked' foot, colic, have prevented him competing at one time and another. In 1973, all set for the International Show in Rome – after winning the BBC Grandstand Trophy at Hickstead, first time out after a six months rest and so easily he did not appear to try – Psalm was kicked in the belly during the first parade in Italy, which virtually put him out of the whole show.

But these are only incidents, unfortunate but passing, in the success story of a horse that, in the happy position of being made and jumped by only one rider, came quickly to the top and looks like remaining there for a long, long time to come. In 1972, before the Olympics, he was often winning more than once at the big shows. It was twice at the Rothman's Lincoln Show Jumping Championships in May, four times at the Devon County in June, as well as at the 'Royal' in July; at Wembley, and of course at Hickstead. And Ann Moore, winning Show Jumper of the Year in '72, is as ambitious as she is dedicated.

With Psalm she won the Women's European Championship in 1971; with the gallant Psalm recovered from his kick only to succumb to equine 'flu and still not on top form, she retained the title and took it for the second successive time in 1973 with a brilliant display of speed jumping in Vienna.

By the 1976 Olympics Psalm will be only fifteen and if all goes well with him and if Ann gets her hoped-for chance, it will be with Psalm that she tries for that coveted Gold Medal to add to their Silver achieved in Munich.

18
PRETTY POLLY

Sooner or later, and sometimes both, the majority of horse and pony champions find themselves included in that parade of equine personalities that is one of the big attractions of the Horse of the Year Show.

In 1970, prominent amongst the well-known characters who were lending their aura to Wembley that year, was a 14-hand chestnut pony with a white stripe and snip on her nose, and a white sock on her off hind. She was not in her first youth and a saddle had been chosen with care to disguise a back dipped with age, but it was obvious from the sparkle in her eyes, from the way she held herself and moved, that she was delighted to be back in an atmosphere very familiar to her, and that in her day she must have been a 'one'.

The first time that pony, called Pretty Polly, had put in an appearance at the Horse of the Year Show was twenty years before, in 1950 when the venue was still Harringay. That day she was heading the line as Children's Pony of the Year, a performance she repeated twelve months later when her brother was second, her sister third.

Pretty Polly was bred in Ireland. Her dam was the little half Welsh, half-Thoroughbred Gypsy Gold, and she was sired by Naseel, that most lovely of all small Arabians, that was bred by the late Lady Yule by Raftan out of Naxina.

In 1949 Polly, then a four-year-old, had been champion at Dublin, and word of her had come to England, to Mr Deptford, the well-known lifelong pony exhibitor and breeder, in 1973 Chairman of the British Pony Society. The accompanying photograph however did the pony small justice, and no move was made until another of Mr Deptford's knowledgeable friends began to extol her, remarking that much as he liked Mr Deptford's Richmond winner, the successful Firefly, he reckoned the little Irish mare would beat her. Then the die was cast.

Polly gave a farewell to Ireland by winning at the Royal Ulster in May, then caught strangles on the boat coming over to England in late June and was out of action for a month. Mr Deptford eventually collected her in July, at the Great Yorkshire where he was exhibiting Firefly.

The pony impressed at once with her obvious quality and beautiful movement, but when stood up beside Firefly, her conformation caused a little doubt. Even in youth Polly had a dip in her back – 'big enough to hold half-a-pint of water' – but six weeks of strapping and massage were to muscle her up along the spine, so that the defect never penalised her during her showing career. In temperament it was immediately apparent that Polly had the edge on Firefly, a difficult character made more so by a previous succession of bad homes.

In theory all show ponies should be suitable for any competent child rider of the correct age for the size of pony, but like many hypotheses the facts too seldom bear out the assumption. Good looks and quality do not necessarily go with good manners, and even show ponies that conform during the actual judging often throw decorum to the winds when loosed off on that exciting 'lap of honour' round the ring.

The 'show condition', essential to success but too often achieved through an abundance of oats, instead of the less heady boiled barley, does not help towards making a pony an easy ride. Sometimes the training for the ring, an art in itself, tends to be skimped, and not all breeders are as meticulous as they might be about the temperament of the dam and sire. But although a judge, faced with a pony of compelling quality and action, might be tempted to turn a blind eye to some idiosyncrasies of behaviour, what that eminent horseman

J.E.Hance was saying way back in the Pretty Polly era in the '50s, is as true today as it was then. And he considered that children's show ponies that misbehave are not 'children's ponies' as such, and that if they do so during the final judging they should not just be relegated down the line, but sent right out of the ring. It is no easy matter to produce a top-class pony for the show ring with the requisite combination of courage and personality with manners, but it can be done and Pretty Polly proved it.

Davina Lee-Smith, a good young rider of much showing experience, exhibited Polly and kept her at her own home in the summer months through the pony's showing career except for Polly's last season when she was ridden by Christine Harries. And although she has been mixed up with show ponies all her life, both before and since those days, Davina acknowledges that she has never met another Polly and doubts if she ever will.

At that time a show pony was seldom expected to do anything else but show, yet that little mare from Ireland could have excelled at almost any pony activity, and unlike the majority of her ilk, would have been the perfect all-round pony for the average child. She was one of those rare animals that really wants to please. Always anxious to do what was required of her to the best of her ability inside the ring and out, she revelled in the fact that she was in luck, and never kept like a piece of delicate china, but within reason was included in the family's every day riding life. She jumped well, and although not hazarded in hunting when the full season started, loved to be taken out for the occasional day's cub-hunting, and always joined with zest in any equestrian games Davina and the other children thought up. Polly was very sound, and except for a skin allergy that kept her away from the Horse of the Year Show in the Coronation Year of 1953, she was never sick or sorry.

The pony had been nicely schooled before making her debut in England, and her training was continued on expert lines. She was taught to go equally well on a circle to either hand, which ensured she would not get into the habit of drifting towards the centre of the ring, and would be sure to strike off on the correct leg when asked. Davina knew all about collecting Polly so that she was both alert and responsive, accepting the bit with proudly arched neck, and her hocks under her, but before very long it was difficult to decide which of them, rider or pony, knew the most about presentation, that vital ingredient of the art of showing. The combination of their talent was to prove virtually unbeatable.

Polly's career in the ring got off with a bang, with a first at Henley-on-Thames on the 23 August. By the time, less than a month later, she made her entrance at Harringay to win, she had collected a 1st at each of the three other shows she attended – the British Timkin at Dunston on 1 September, Buck's County on 7 September, Northants County on 9 September – and her rider had come to know and appreciate the pony's endearing qualities.

Pretty Polly genuinely loved showing. Even with two, sometimes three shows in a week she was never to become stale, and like the Strollers and Arkles of this world she was a superb showman. At just on 14 hands she was small for her class, but used to enter with all the panache of a true *prima donna*, carrying herself so that she 'grew' to match the other competitors. She was always eager to oblige and to put on the best show possible, and although displaying the required fire and grace, never under any circumstances forgot her manners.

Polly always seemed to know when the competition was particularly 'hot', the times when she and Davina had their 'backs to the wall', so to speak. These were the occasions when she pulled out that little bit extra, and used to fix the judges with her wonderfully expressive eye, appearing to challenge them to take notice of her and acknowledge her beauty with the appropriate trophy. These tactics, when she was averaging eighteen or nineteen shows a year in her three seasons in the ring, only failed once, when she was beaten by Royal Show. Otherwise she took first prize in the class for ponies not exceeding 14.2 hands, at every show she attended, and collected championships almost as a matter of course.

Polly, fully aware of her own worth and triumphs, always demanded her due once the competing was finished, and if the ice-cream she adored was not immediately forthcoming, would stamp on the floor of her trailer until it was.

This pony's phenomenal success in the show ring was due in part to the fact that she was trained, produced and ridden by experts. But the good basic material that is an essential to work on, the quality, action, substance and temperament, was a product of good breeding. The superlative, as opposed to the very good pony, is a rarity, and although it does sometimes appear by chance, more often it is the product of knowledge and judgement in choosing the right stallion for the right mare. Even then there is certainly no guarantee of success, and there is also the unknown factor, that however well matched by ancestry and physical attributes ponies may appear to be, with one sire the mare may produce good or indifferent foals, with another of apparently no greater merit, she may found a dynasty.

Pretty Polly's mother, Gypsy Gold, obviously found exactly the right mate in Naseel, and when Mr Deptford imported Polly's younger and smaller sister, My Pretty Maid, she competed with almost equal success in the 13.2 hand classes. There was also a full brother, Eureka, that was not shown as extensively as his sisters, but did marvellously well in the larger classes.

When Pretty Polly was retired to stud, at the pinnacle of her showing career – and after taking her revenge and beating Royal Show, the only animal ever to relegate her to second place – great care was taken over the choice of stallions to try to ensure her a comparable triumph as a brood mare. Polly responded through the years by producing eleven foals that were all champions bar one, but even so she had her preferences, and the most famous of her celebrated family were sired by one particular stallion.

She had a lovely first foal by the Pure-bred Arabian, Count Dorsaz, but the second, by Blue Domino, although handsome and sweet natured, was the one to break her record of champion children because he grew too big to be shown. So next time Polly went to the Welsh pony, Bolged Automation, which assured an offspring of the right size and produced Cusop Policy and after that found her perfect mate, the legendary pony sire, Bwlch Valentino.

This handsome grey, that with his sons is largely responsible for the characteristic sweeping action of the modern riding pony, possessed Arabian, Welsh and Thoroughbred blood, and between them he and Pretty Polly bred the most beautiful and successful show ponies that, in their turn are carrying on the family line of champions.

There was one tragedy, a fine colt foal that died of tetanus, and regrettably, for physical reasons, the lovely little Jenny Wren, a champion in her own right, could not be used for breeding. Polly Perkins was another daughter that won fame and fortune, and Polly's Gem was the dam of three champions that included Gem's Signet, a grand-daughter that was Champion Riding Pony in 1972. But perhaps the most famous of Pretty Polly's and Valentino's family was Pollyanna, now in America and breeding a line of champions there, to perpetuate Pretty Polly's name on the other side of the Atlantic.

Pollyanna was shown once or twice as a three-year-old in 1961, but blossomed in all her glory as a four-year-old to follow in her mother's footsteps, by winning classes and championships alike, and becoming Champion Riding Pony of the Year at Harringay in that same season.

This little mare inherited her mother's temperament as well as her looks and presence, and she was sold to America for the then record price of £6,000. Unfortunately there was not much opportunity to show the pony in suitable classes around her new home in the midwest, but when she again came on the market in 1966 she was bought by a Mrs Waller, who had been keeping track of the pony ever since seeing her in England.

By then Pollyanna had no show record in the States and the original intention was to use her straight away at stud. But after a few months the pony regained all her old showing presence, and returned to the ring. American classes are unlike those in Britain, and in the majority the ponies have to jump, and instead of being collected, go on a loose rein with heads carried in a relaxed position. But Pollyanna was as versatile as her mother and in the new venue won many championships for her new owners, culminating with the supreme championship at New York's Madison Square Garden, the show that then carried the most prestige for ponies in all America.

All told, the children and grand-children of Pretty Polly and Bwlch Valentino have carved out a fine record, but as the years passed the mare did not always get in foal and it was decided to try a younger sire. The choice fell on Bwlch Zephyr, one of Valentino's sons, also a grey, that was supreme champion at the Ponies of Britain stallion show in 1966, and himself the sire of many champions. Again the selection proved a happy one, and before she retired to the honoured status of elderly matriarch, Polly bred some more beautiful fillies.

Pretty Polly was still alive early in 1973. At twenty-eight and the mother of eleven, the old back, no longer muscled up, sagged a bit, the chestnut coat was long and shaggy, and maybe there was a twinge of rheumatism, but the little head was still lovely, with that eloquent eye defying old age, and the pony that had been the darling of Mr Deptford's heart for so many years, was still obviously enjoying life. In winter she had the day-time run of the big yard at his farm where she could exercise in the shelter of the buildings, in the summer she inhabited the same field, close by the house, where for year after year she used to bring the current foal each morning up to the gate, for the express purpose of showing off this latest offspring and to say a friendly 'good-morning'.

Now Pretty Polly is dead: she became ill and was put down in April 1973, but as the prototype of the perfect show-pony, in looks, manners and personality, and as the mother of a line that carries on the same traditions, she will never be forgotten.

19
IMPERIAL

In 1760 a mounted horse patrol was the core of a 'Plan' for the 'Suppression of Highwaymen, Footpads, Housebreakers and Other Offenders'. Now, more than 200 years later and well into the technologically marvellous space age, in numerous countries throughout the world police horses are still a recognised and effective arm of the law.

In cities as large and up to date as Sydney and Tokyo, London and New York, the horses are actively engaged in keeping the peace, as well as being used for the more obvious ceremonial duties. For while the presence of the beautifully turned-out and mannered horses with their smart riders, must always add to the pageantry and colour of a ceremonial occasion or traditional parade, there is, too, the great asset that the majority of people retain an innate and healthy respect for a horse. And this is one of several reasons why in recent years, the Mounted Branch of the Metropolitan Police in London have become even more involved in crowd control. It is also, combined with the shortage of man-power, why the horses are being employed more often as a normal part of policing rather than in the role of a reserve force. During 1971 the Mounted Branch were responsible for more than one hundred arrests, around 3,500 summonses, and nearly 4,000 verbal warnings.

All police horses therefore are champions of the law, and through the years a few have also qualified for the most honoured duty any champion could undertake, acting as ceremonial chargers for the Queen at her annual official birthday parade, the Trooping the Colour.

To this category belonged Imperial, a 16.0 hand, three-quarter-bred chestnut, with a white face and four white stockings, that was bought by the Metropolitan Mounted Branch as an unbroken three-year-old in 1955. Nowadays the Force has a new policy of internal breeding, on a limited scale, but then, with the exception of the animals presented as gifts, the majority of the horses, like Imperial, came from Yorkshire.

The gelding was sent straight to Imber Court, the Metropolitan Police training centre in Surrey, for the six month's basic education that all their horses receive. And here, like all the young remounts, Imperial was in the charge of one of the permanent training staff. Men well experienced in the breaking and schooling of young animals who each take on two at a time, and are chosen for a combination of patience, firmness and ability. As far as possible they are also given horses to which they are temperamentally suited.

For the first six weeks Imperial was schooled with the trainer working from the ground. He was driven on long reins and taught to obey vocal commands, and the first weight he felt on his back was a driving pad, followed by a 'dumb jockey', a somewhat old-fashioned but effective contraption, with crossed 'arms' that waggle with the movement of the horse and give it some idea of the feel of a rider. The chestnut had a kind, if essentially gay temperament, but the entire training programme at Imber Court is geared to keeping the young horses calm and relaxed and therefore responsive to what is required of them. It is based on a system of reward, with the oat bowl always in evidence, and co-operation soon acquires a pleasurable association.

After some weeks Imperial was 'backed' without any undue fuss on his part, and from then on the pattern of training was extended to include the special requirements of a police horse. He had, of necessity, to become absolutely traffic proof and since a mounted policeman must be able to forget his horse and concentrate on whatever duty is in hand, he had to become instantly obedient to his rider's aids. As time wore on Imperial learned to jump and to cope with diversions such as going up and down steps, both accomplishments that improve a horse's versatility, and almost from the start he was given lessons in 'nuisance' training. This entailed an early introduction to such objects as furled flags and umbrellas, with a few oats always to hand to induce indifference. Soon he would work quietly in the school with a 'ride', at trot and canter, circling, changing the rein and performing half-passes, all done to the fiendish accompaniment of shouts, gun-fire and brass bands produced from a loud speaker at full volume. With the other pupils Imperial learned to stand on a loose rein, unmoved while flags and umbrellas, by then unfurled, were waved in their faces, and to ignore the ear-splitting clamour of those 'rattles' beloved of football fans, the clanging of fire-bells and the staccato crackle of revolvers fired close at hand. He was taught to step over 'bodies' lying in his path, and to accept people clinging to railings or perched on walls above his head as all part of the normal scene. He had to push his way between dummies, or shoulder back another set mounted on wheels – preliminary to shoving against a posse of instructors acting as the rowdies who sometimes attempt to upend a police horse.

Imperial took it all in his stride, and while retaining his innate gaiety, showed early signs of becoming one of the 'stars' of Imber Court. Then came the day when, his initial training completed, he left for the stables at Great Scotland Yard to start on the further education 'on the beat', that produces an experienced police horse.

All the novice horses are teamed up with experienced riders, while the 'old hands' take care of, and frequently 'take the mickey' out of, the novice policemen. For the first years Imperial was looked after and ridden by Constable Varley, an accomplished horseman and expert at bringing on young horses, and he quickly became a reliable animal, always friendly with people, and well versed in the work required of him. Each day, except for Sunday (unless there was an exceptional call on the mounted police on that day), Imperial did the normal three hours out on patrol. He learned to accept calmly any duty from traffic control to the direction of the crowd gathered to watch the Changing of the Guard at Buckingham Palace; from the energetic escorting of a new ambassador being driven at the trot to present his credentials to the Queen, to helping preserve the peace in the comparative tranquility of one of the royal parks.

Imperial also proved a versatile and successful participant on those enjoyable occasions when the mounted police further good public relations by competing, usually in special classes at some of the larger shows, and Constable Varley and his handsome horse became well-known figures at venues such as Richmond. Several times Imperial had the distinction of acting as leading file for the well-known Musical Ride the mounted police put on at their annual show at Imber Court, and he was ridden there also by the Chief Equitation Instructor.

When Constable Varley was once more required to use his talents on a less experienced horse, Imperial became the mount of Superintendent Denton and some of his duties then altered slightly in character. He was ridden to supervise mounted patrols and inspect other police stables in Inner London, and attended every possible ceremonial occasion. Once he took a leading part in the type of demonstration that was rare in those days but is only too familiar in these. A big crowd, gathered in front of the Houses of Parliament was withstanding all efforts of the foot police to disperse them. As was usual practice then, the horses were being held strictly in reserve, but a request for help brought the superintendent and Imperial to the scene, leading a squad of nineteen mounted police. By then the crowd were in an increasingly ugly mood and groups of foot police had become isolated. A show of force would have been worse than useless if it had proved ineffective, and the Inspector waited for the arrival of twenty reinforcements. Then he wheeled Imperial to head his posse, and advanced slowly and steadily towards the threatening demonstrators.

This is the moment when a police horse needs all his background of careful training. Horses are very sensitive to human emotions, particularly those generated by an excited, unruly crowd. There was uproar and anger, the threat of clenched fists and waving arms, and many to attempt to press forwards instead of back, but neither Imperial nor any of the horses wavered, and as the line of forty animals came steadily on, so the crowd gradually faltered, and broke up, and the situation was once more under control.

By this time Imperial was not only a first-class police horse in his normal duties, he was also a very famous and well-known animal at the highest level. The mounted police always keep an eye out amongst their remounts, for any likely candidates for eventual inclusion in the dozen or so horses yearly provided for Service Chiefs and members of the royal household at the Trooping the Colour. From these they choose two or three of the best that might ultimately be good enough to carry the Queen, and Imperial was an early qualifier for this honour. Looks are of some importance, and the horse must be sufficiently large and impressive to have the bearing of a royal charger, and be of a colour to set off the uniform and catch the eye. Imperial certainly fulfilled these requirements, he possessed even more quality than Winston, his famous predecessor, but in the earliest days there was some small doubt about temperament — by far the most important requirement. For while the Queen's charger should not be so quiet that it is indifferent to what is going on, and therefore more liable to be startled by a sudden noise or disturbance, equally it has to be sufficiently calm to behave perfectly on the route lined by vast and cheering crowds between the Palace and Horse Guard's Parade, and then to stand motionless throughout the larger part of an hour-long exciting military ceremony.

Imperial was always full of the spirit that his breeding and colour would suggest. He could resent too much intensive schooling, and needed always to be ridden with the tact that the Queen instinctively brings to her riding. With a less sympathetic rider he had been known to play up and even throw a hefty buck. But though, as the Queen remarked, in the indoor school at Buckingham Palace the chestnut could pull harder than any horse she had ridden, on parade he was superb.

Throughout the year Superintendent Denton and Imperial used to attend numerous public occasions, and unlike some police horses that combine good work on the beat with an unconquerable distaste for the trappings of ceremonial, this horse obviously enjoyed the big occasions and liked to be the centre of attention. He put in two appearances in the Personality Parade at the Horse of the Year Show, each time bearing himself with an impressive dignity suited to his status and the event, and was happy to receive the adulation —

and sweets – that usually came his way from at least some members of the public when he was on street patrol.

There are not many horses that would back quietly and obediently between the ranks of the pipes and drums of a military band. Yet Mrs Archer-Houblon, the lady who came annually to school Imperial in a side-saddle for a few weeks before the Trooping, was able to do just that, and to persuade him to stand motionless in position when the band then struck up with a terrific roll of drums. Nor did Imperial ever hesitate in that exacting moment before the Trooping, when the Queen leaves the Palace out in front of her escort and her horse has to move on alone, under the centre archway, into the forecourt, and so to face the cheering, the great wave of emotional sound that seems like an almost tangible barrier.

Except for a few weeks of extra schooling prior to the Trooping, Imperial received no specialised training. Each year the Queen, always meticulous in everything she does, rides for an hour on most days for a month beforehand in the covered school at the Palace, re-newing her partnership with the most likely horses, and limbering muscles only used in this form of riding once a year. The police always have at least two suitable 'understudies' in readiness – in fact the Queen only makes her final choice of horse on the evening before the ceremony – and these are brought round for the Queen to meet, and for her, and in those days Mrs Archer-Houblon, to try.

As is usual Imperial was always ridden at both the Trooping rehearsals, and then it would be the big day itself when, early in the morning he would be taken from Great Scotland Yard to the Royal Mews, for a final grooming of his shining coat before being accoutred. Then his police bridle, complete with the chains that can be clipped to the bit should the leather reins be cut through by some hooligan, was exchanged for the royal ceremonial bridle, complete with blue browband and rosettes. Under the beautifully tooled side-saddle with its single gold-gilt stirrup, he wore the blue saddlecloth embroidered in gold, and over all went a waterproof saddle cover to be left in position while he was led round to the Inner Quadrangle at the Palace.

This is where the Queen's escort wait; Gold-Stick-in-Waiting, Silver-Stick-in-Waiting, the Equerries-in-Waiting to Her Majesty,

Colonels and Lieutenant-Colonels and Adjutants of the Regiments of Foot Guards, the Major-General Commanding London District, four troopers of the Life Guards and two grooms of the royal household, all drawn up on the south side. This is where the two barouches, each drawn by a pair of Windsor Greys, stand ready to take the Queen Mother and other members of the royal family to the parade ground. This is where footmen place mounting blocks in front of the King's Door, where the Master of Horse and the Crown Equerry stand to greet the Queen, and where the horses are held, in those years usually Imperial for the Queen, Linnhe, a big mare from Cannon Row for Prince Philip, and the grand old Fairway for the Duke of Gloucester.

With precise timing the Queen and her husband come down the steps from the King's Door. She wears the attractive, adapted uniform of a Colonel-in-Chief of one of the regiments of Foot Guards. There's a greeting for everyone, a pat for her horse, — by his expression Imperial was always hoping this was the moment for the tit-bit he would receive after the parade — then while grooms flick at imaginary specks on bits and bridles, the Crown Equerry aids the Queen to mount, and Prince Philip gets astride his horse. There are gay asides and laughter, in those years a wave for Prince Andrew, then a little boy standing at a window to watch, and the Queen wheels her horse and rides out, a brave figure, once more to take part in a colourful tradition of military pageantry.

That was the duty that for many years crowned Imperial's career as a policehorse. He always appeared to understand the honour and to take great pride in being *the* horse of the occasion, and in all the time he carried the Queen at her Birthday Parade his bearing and manners remained impeccable. In the end unsoundness, his feet were always a weakness, led to his preclusion and eventually he had to be put down. But all through his life, whether he was patrolling the London streets upholding the law, or whether he was taking on the proud role of royal charger, Imperial was an acknowledged champion.

20

ALBATROSS

A four-horse chariot race was included in the twenty-third Olympiad in 688 BC, but it was to be more than 2,000 years before harness racing, as such, became popular in America, the cradle of the modern sport.

In the New World its origins lie not in any organised contest but in the expansion of a man's competative instinct to prove his horse a faster, better trotter than that of his neighbour. And since horse-drawn carts and carriages were the everyday and universal means of transport, this form of 'racing' appeared more democratic and, to the Puritanical, far less sinful than the so-called 'sport of Kings', indulged solely as a leisure pastime and associated with the loose goings-on of the wealthier classes.

Harness racing continued to prosper until the advent of the motor-car drove it temporarily into the shadows – in common with a number of other simple joys of life. When the sport re-emerged from the more remote areas where it had been kept alive during the Second World War, it soon ceased to be the unsophisticated pastime of purely country folk. Boosted by floodlit racing at night, with all the modern amenities of the huge metropolitan racing plants at its disposal, and with the pockets of the post war enthusiasts positively bulging with betting money, harness racing rapidly developed into the top-line sport it is today. A sport that has become equally popular in Austra-lasia, Russia and the majority of European countries, but has only just started to awaken real interest in Britain.

The original American trotters were horses of varied origins whose only qualification was their trotting ability and even when a register was established it was based on performance rather than breeding. Then gradually the emphasis came on blood lines as well, until a recognised and highly standardised breed was evolved. It was called the Standardbred, because the object of the breeding was to produce a harness racer capable of 'doing the mile' within the limits of a pre-scribed standard of time.

The modern Standardbred averages about 15.2 hands and looks very like a longer and sturdier type of Thoroughbred. In fact Stan-ardbreds trace back on the male line to a grey Thoroughbred race-horse called Messenger, that was foaled in Britain in 1780 and arrived in Philadelphia eight years later. Messenger's great-grandson was a horse named Hambledonian, and from the direct descendants of four distinguished sons of this animal come ninety-nine per cent of all American Harness racers, trotters and pacers alike.

The trotter moves the opposite front and hind legs forward so that they strike the ground in a rhythmical one-two-beat involving the alternate pairs of legs, a peak development of the traditional roadster's gait which at its best has been described as much like a barrel rolling straight down a hill. There are two basic types, the line-gaited trotter that trots straight and the passing-gaited where the hind leg comes slightly outside the front leg.

The pacer moves like a camel, his same-side legs pistoning back-wards and forwards in unison, and the constant shifting of his weight from the right side to the left and back again, produces the typical rocking, rolling motion, quite different from that of the trotter whose body is always balanced in the centre. In medieval England 'ambling' horses that performed an unexaggerated, smooth and gliding version of the modern pace, were much sought after for the comfort of their gail on long journeys, but even they were usually taught this gait with the aid of rope 'hobbles'.

Originally the pacer was very much the poor relation of the trotter and scarcely recognised until 1855 when the speedy exploits of the great pacing mare, Pocahantas, aroused some public interest. Twenty-four years later due to the thrilling track battles waged between four brilliant exponents of the art, the pacers came to be tolerated. Yet within living memory they were still objects of disdain to the majority of harness racers, principally because the pacing gait is an acquired one, and pacers are almost always fitted with the 'hopples' (or hobbles) that help them to maintain the gait in situations where they would otherwise by very likely to 'break'. The pace is therefore considered an artificial gait – although in fact, since the gallop is the natural pace of the horse at speed, this applies also to trotters – and even though nowadays pacers bred to each other almost without exception produce pacing offspring, and often do so if mated to a trotter. Nor is it unknown for two trotters to produce a pacer!

In the end the undeniable speed of the pacer removed any need of a champion, and today the 'sidewheeler' or pacer is the most popular animal on the harness racing tracks. A change of opinion well and truly borne out in 1972 when the brilliant young pacer, Albatross, gained 136 votes out of 191 to make him champion Harness Horse of the Year, in addition to his other titles of Pacer of the Year, and the award of Best Four-Year-Old Pacer of the Year for which he collected every vote bar one.

The story of this pacing prodigy really began on the day Bert Vansickle James, an automobile dealer in Windsor, Ontario, accepted three harness racing horses as part payment for a Cadillac. One of the animals did him so well that first racing, and then breeding Standardbreds became his hobby, and when he sold his business in 1965 and leased a farm, these interests became his life work. He says he remains basically a business man, but horses plus that business acumen have done him well. He lives in Pittsburgh, and Albatross has a lot to do with the fact that Bert Vansickle James is now a millionaire.

The horse, by Meadow Skipper, was acquired early in 1969 as part of a package deal, priced at $11,000, that included his dam, Voodoo Hanover. The mare was the object of the exercise, and James had small interest in her yearling colt and its suckling sister. In fact his first impulse was to sell the colt and recoup his expenditure, but his luck held. No-one would offer him his price and so the yearling was christened Albatross and sent to Harry Harvey, a colt man of reputation, to be trained.

At that stage Albatross would have been quiet to handle. Pacers are usually taught to lead at two days old, by following their mother and with a line round the rump as encouragement. And since the shoeing and balance of trotters and pacers is inter-related the former is a complicated science with an infinity of different shoes for the different gaits for an infinity of different reasons. All harness racers have endless dates with the blacksmith, and so at an equally tender age a foal is taught to pick up his feet as required. Apart from such basic good manners, a pacer such as Albatross would have a great deal to learn between his introduction to Harry Harvey, and their first tryout on the track towards the end of May in the following year.

He may have been already partially broken in, although this is not done with the majority until they are eighteen months old, when they are physically strong enough and mentally able — if inevitably still youthfully self-willed — to learn what is required from a trainer with the requisite patience and skill.

Albatross had first to learn to be tied, by gradual degrees, until he would stand calmly held by the chain crossties. He had to become accustomed to a bridle, and although some horses are later trained and raced in an 'open' bridle, that is without blinkers, the first is usually a 'blind' one so that the young animal cannot see behind him and become frightened by the rest of his harness. This usually consists of a crupper, the soft strap that goes under the tail, and the overcheck, the strap running from between the colt's ears to the top of the driving saddle, that is first fitted loosely, and is an indispensable aid to driving a harness racer. When he was happy with the harness Albatross was line-driven, with his trainer walking behind and handling the long lines, and with, for a start, an assistant postioned in front and slightly to the left, with another line as an emergency hand-brake.

The next step was to hitch Albatross to a training cart and drive him. From that big moment the lessons continued each day, until he was drawing a proper racing sulky, and at some stage had been introduced to the hobbles that are worn by pacers to steady them and help them maintain the gait. Each nobble consists of two light plastic and nylon loops, with an adjustable strap between, that go loosely around the fore and hind legs on the same side, and are held in place with body straps. They are adjusted according to the needs of each individual pacer, so that his stride just 'fills' the loop. If it were not for the number of big races involving a lot of mone y that are now run over the half mile at a single dash, instead of with the customary three or more heats, and if so much big money was not connected with the racing of two and three-year-olds, there could be many more horses racing as natural, free-legged pacers. But the short 'dash' requires hobbles to keep the pacer from breaking on the turns, and in the second instance the youth of the animal does not allow the time necessary for making a good, free-legged pacer, and so the hobbles provide the necessary short cut.

It was not long before Albatross was well broken and ready for the training routine. And that follows a pattern, with each trainer's variations thrown in, of giving each horse the right feed and the right amount of work to make him fit and hard and keep that way. It involves teaching him the procedure and requirements of the track and, certainly not least, developing the same kind of rapport between horse and driver that a jockey and his Thoroughbred also need to produce the best results.

The two-year-old Albatross and Harry Harvey made their racing debut on 20 May 1970, in a 'baby' race. They won in an impressive 2 minutes $7\frac{2}{5}$ seconds but public interest was occupied with the deeds of other, well-known horses, and both that and Albatross's succeeding win passed almost unnoticed. It was a different matter by the time he had completed his season as a two-year-old. By then he had won his first, and his last four consecutive races, had filled the interim between with nothing less than a third place, and in Canada had clocked up a fantastic 1 minute $57\frac{4}{5}$ seconds in the second division of Vernon Downs Grand Circuit stake. He was voted Two-Year-Old Pacer of the Year by the United States Trotting Association, and proclaimed Horse of the Year by their Canadian counterpart.

Albatross was kept in light training during that winter, and amused himself in his off time by kicking the sides of his stall, specially padded for the purpose. In April 1971 he was syndicated for both racing and future breeding by a nine-member group, with his owner James the principal share-holder. The price – $1,250,000.

For purely business reasons this necessitated Albatross leaving Harry Harvey to be trained and driven by Stanley Dancer, the most famous name in American harness racing today. Again, in the capable hands of his new partner, the colt dominated the tracks, hard surface or soft alike, tearing off the vital seconds with the piston-rhythm of his devastating stride, and finishing up that incredible season by beating all the finest pacers in the country to take the $100,000 American Pacing Classic.

Well might Stanley Dancer rate the Big Bird, as the horse was nicknamed, the greatest pacer he had ever raced and the best gaited pacer he had ever seen. The next season more than confirmed his opinion, and was shared by all the thousands of enthusiasts who watched Albatross flashing down the many tracks he raced on, to clock up win after win. It was a conviction proved beyond all doubt on that incredible day when this horse not only went one mile in 1 minute $54\frac{4}{5}$ seconds but did the two miles, or heats, in exactly the same time. No other pacer had ever achieved two miles, back to back, each in 1 minute $54\frac{4}{5}$ seconds and as though to emphasise his superiority, at the moment when he was streaking down the Lexington straight towards his record, Albatross leaped high in the air – without breaking his stride.

Albatross was retired to stud at Hanover Shoe Farms at the end of his 1972 season. And before Stanley Dancer took his Big Bird on the exhibition jog in front of a 5,000 strong crowd, gathered at Dover Downs to do their champion homage, Albatross had won in a single season more prize money than any other harness horse, and had established himself as the fastest racing Standardbred in the history of the sport.